KAWASAKI

SERVICE・REPAIR HANDBOOK

250 & 350cc Twins・All Years

Published by

CLYMER PUBLICATIONS

*World's largest publisher of books devoted exclusively to
automobiles, motorcycles, and boats.*

222 NORTH VIRGIL AVENUE, LOS ANGELES, CALIFORNIA 90004

FIRST EDITION
First Printing November, 1972
Second Printing April, 1974
Third Printing March, 1976
Fourth Printing October, 1977

Printed in U.S.A.

ISBN: 0-89287-016-8

MTA
MEMBER

MIC
MOTORCYCLE INDUSTRY COUNCIL

CONTENTS

CHAPTER ONE

GENERAL INFORMATION

INTRODUCTION

This book was written to help you, the owner, service and repair your Kawasaki twin-cylinder motorcycle. The information in this book applies to the following machines.

A1	A7
A1SS	A7SS
A1R	A7R

SERVICE HINTS

Most of the service procedures described are straightforward, and can be performed by anyone reasonably handy with tools. It is suggested, however, that you consider your own capabilities carefully before attempting any operation which involves major disassembly of the engine.

Some procedures, for example, require the use of a press. It would be wiser to have those performed by a shop equipped for such work, rather than to try it with makeshift equipment. Other maintenance requires precision measurements. Unless you have the skills and equipment needed, it would be better to have a motorcycle shop make them for you.

Repairs will be much faster and easier if your machine is clean before you begin work. There are special cleaners for washing the engine and related parts. Just brush or spray on the cleaning solution, let it stand, then rinse away with a garden hose.

Clean all oily or greasy parts with cleaning solvent as you remove them. **Never use gasoline as a cleaning agent.** It presents an extreme fire hazard. Be sure to work in a well-ventilated area when using any solvent. Have a fire extinguisher, rated for gasoline fires, handy just in case.

Special tools are required for some service procedures. These may be purchased at Kawasaki dealers. If you are on good terms with the dealer's service department, you may be able to borrow tools occasionally.

Much of a dealer's labor charge for repairs covers preliminary removal and disassembly to reach a defective part. It is frequently possible to do all this yourself, then take the affected subassembly into the shop for repair.

Once you decide to tackle a job yourself, read the entire section in this manual pertaining to it. Study the illustrations and the text until you have a good idea of what is involved. If special tools are required, make arrangements to get them **before** you start the job. It's frustrating to get partly into a repair and then find yourself unable to complete it.

TOOLS

To properly service your bike, an assortment

of ordinary hand tools will be required. Be sure to have the following:

1. Combination wrenches
2. Socket wrenches
3. Plastic mallet
4. Small hammer
5. Snap ring pliers
6. Phillips screwdrivers
7. Pliers
8. Slot screwdrivers
9. Feeler gauges
10. Spark plug gauge
11. Spark plug wrench
12. Dial indicator

A tool kit suitable for most minor servicing is shown in **Figure 1**. It's available through Kawasaki dealers.

Electrical system servicing requires a voltmeter, ohmmeter or other device for determining continuity; and a hydrometer for battery checking. The hydrometer is inexpensive, and should be part of every motorcyclist's tool kit.

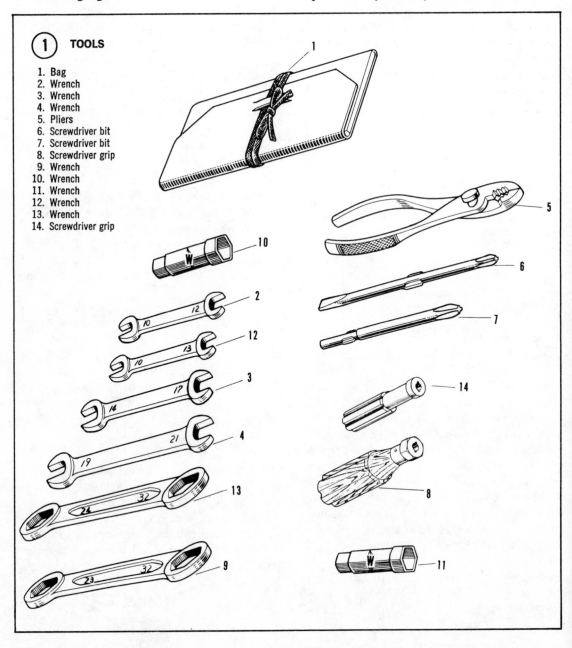

① TOOLS

1. Bag
2. Wrench
3. Wrench
4. Wrench
5. Pliers
6. Screwdriver bit
7. Screwdriver bit
8. Screwdriver grip
9. Wrench
10. Wrench
11. Wrench
12. Wrench
13. Wrench
14. Screwdriver grip

EXPENDABLE SUPPLIES

Certain expendable supplies are also required. These include grease, oil, gasket cement, wiping rags, cleaning solvent, and distilled water. Cleaning solvent is available at many service stations and auto supply outlets. Distilled water for the battery is available at every supermarket. It is sold for use in steam irons.

SAFETY FIRST

Professional motorcycle mechanics can work for years and never sustain a serious injury. If you observe a few rules of common sense and safety, you can enjoy many safe hours servicing your own machine. You can also hurt yourself or damage your machine if you ignore these rules.

1. Never use gasoline as a cleaning solvent.

2. Never smoke or use a torch in the area of flammable liquids, such as cleaning solvent, kept in open containers.

3. Never smoke or use a torch in an area where batteries are charging. Highly explosive hydrogen gas is formed during the charging process.

4. If welding or brazing is required, remove the fuel tank to a safe distance, at least 50 feet away.

5. Be sure to use the proper size wrenches for nut turning.

6. If a nut is tight, think for a moment what would happen to your hand should the wrench slip. Be guided accordingly.

7. Keep your work area clean and uncluttered.

8. Wear safety goggles in all operations involving drilling, grinding, or use of a chisel.

9. Do not use worn tools.

10. Keep a fire extinguisher handy. Be sure it is rated for gasoline and electrical fires.

CHAPTER TWO

ENGINE, TRANSMISSION, AND CLUTCH

This chapter describes removal, disassembly, service, and reassembly of the engine, transmission, and clutch. It is suggested that the engine be serviced without removing it from the chassis except for overhaul of the crankshaft assembly, transmission, gearshift mechanism, or bearings. Operating principles of rotary valve two-stroke engines are also discussed in this chapter. Kawasaki twin-cylinder machines are equipped with rotary valves.

ENGINE PRINCIPLES

Figures 1 through 4 illustrate the four phases of the operating cycle. During this discussion, assume that the crankshaft is rotating counter-clockwise. In **Figure 1**, as the piston travels downward, a transfer, or scavenging, port (A) is opened. The exhaust gases leave the cylinder through the exhaust port (B), which is also opened by the downward movement of the piston (C). A fresh fuel/air charge, which has previously been compressed, travels from the crankcase (C) through the scavenging port (A) as the port opens.

Figure 2 illustrates the next phase in the cycle. As the crankshaft rotates, the piston moves upward, closing the exhaust and scavenging ports. The fresh fuel/air mixture is trapped in the cylinder and compressed by the upward movement

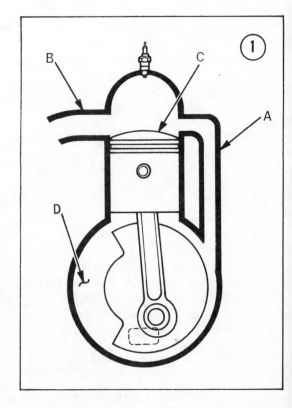

of the piston. Notice also that a low pressure area is created in the crankcase as the piston moves upward. The rotary valve (E), which is attached to the crankshaft and rotates with it, opens the intake port (F). The upward move-

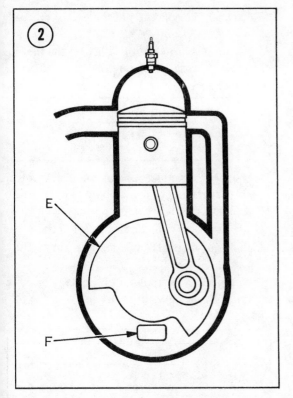

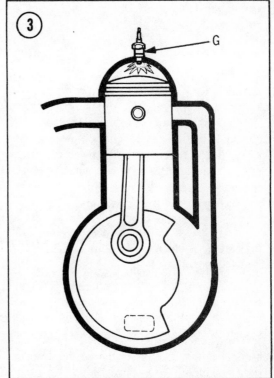

2

ment of the piston then draws a fresh fuel/air charge into the crankcase through the intake port.

The third phase is shown in **Figure 3**. As the piston approaches top dead center, the spark plug (G) fires, igniting the mixture. The piston is then driven downward by the expanding gases. The rotary valve also closes at the time the piston reaches top dead center. As the piston continues downward, the mixture in the crankcase is compressed.

When the piston uncovers the exhaust port, the fourth phase begins, as shown in **Figure 4**. The exhaust gases leave the cylinder through the exhaust port. Further movement of the piston opens the scavenging port, and the cycle is then repeated.

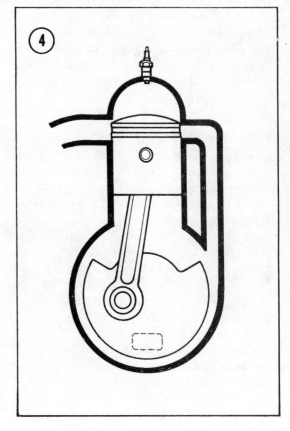

ENGINE LUBRICATION

A conventional two-stroke engine cannot receive its lubrication from an oil supply in the crankcase. Oil splash in the crankcase would be carried into the cylinder with the fuel/air charge, resulting in high oil consumption and spark plug fouling. Kawasaki twin-cylinder engines use one of two methods for engine lubrication.

Superlube System

This system is used on A1 series machines. A separate engine-driven oil pump (**Figure 5**) supplies lubricating oil from an oil tank to the engine induction tract. The output from the pump is controlled not only by engine speed, but also by throttle position, which is closely related to engine load. Therefore, the engine is supplied with the proper amount of oil under all operating conditions.

Injectolube System

The Injectolube system used on A7 series models, is similar to the Superlube system in that it supplies oil to the engine in varying quantities to meet the engine needs. The oil pump has an additional output, however, which supplies oil under pressure to the main and connecting rod bearings (**Figure 6**) in the engine.

OIL PUMP

Figure 7 illustrates a typical oil pump. The pump is a precision assembly; never attempt to disassemble it. Should a malfunction occur, replace it.

To check the condition of the pump, proceed as follows:

1. Mix sufficient two-stroke oil with the fuel in the tank to produce an approximate 15 to 1 mixture.

Fuel	Oil
1 gallon	2 ounces
4 liters	250 cubic centimeters

2. Remove the outlet pipe at the check· valve. Connect the outlet from the pump to a collecting vessel by means of a suitable piece of tubing.

3. Start the engine and run it at 2,000 rpm.

4. Pull the control lever on the pump fully upward.

5. Measure the quantity of oil pumped in three minutes. Proper quantities are listed in the following table:

Series	Oil Quantity	
	Ounces	Cubic Centimeters
A1	0.13-0.16	3.9-4.6
A7	0.16-0.19	4.7-5.5

Oil Pump Adjustment

The oil pump is controlled by throttle position, and therefore must be adjusted after any change in throttle cable adjustment.

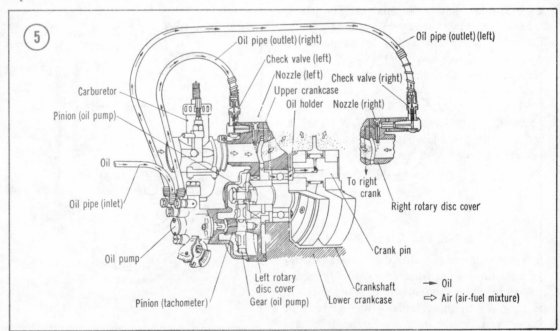

⑤ Carburetor — Pinion (oil pump) — Oil — Oil pipe (inlet) — Oil pump — Pinion (tachometer) — Left rotary disc cover — Gear (oil pump) — Lower crankcase — Crankshaft — Crank pin — Right rotary disc cover — To right crank — Nozzle (right) — Oil holder — Upper crankcase — Check valve (right) — Nozzle (left) — Check valve (left) — Oil pipe (outlet) (right) — Oil pipe (outlet) (left)
→ Oil   ⇨ Air (air-fuel mixture)

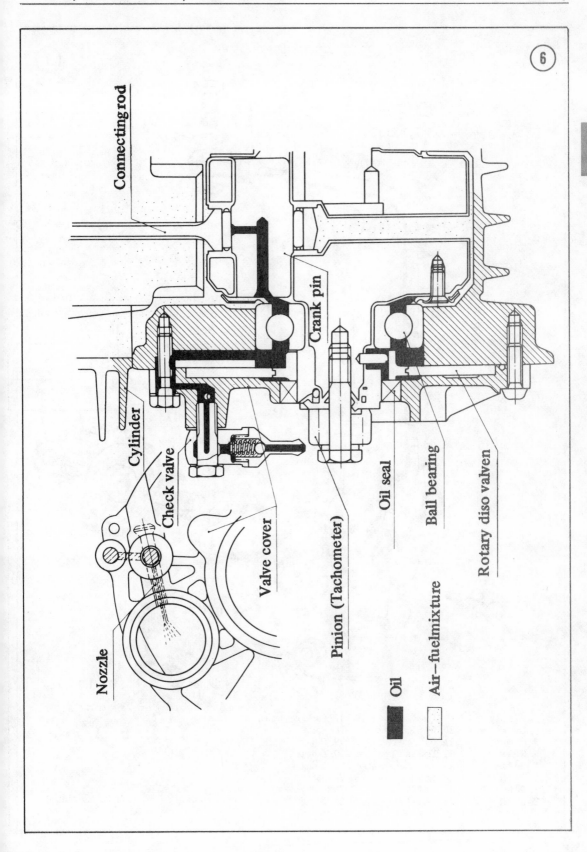

Connecting rod

Crank pin

Cylinder

Check valve

Nozzle

Valve cover

Pinion (Tachometer)

Oil seal

Ball bearing

Rotary diso valven

Oil

Air–fuelmixture

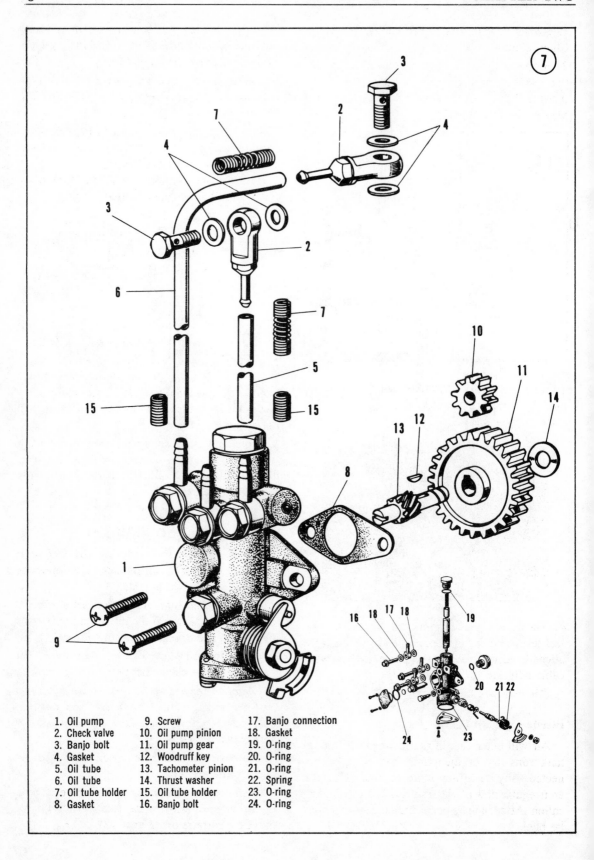

1. Oil pump
2. Check valve
3. Banjo bolt
4. Gasket
5. Oil tube
6. Oil tube
7. Oil tube holder
8. Gasket

9. Screw
10. Oil pump pinion
11. Oil pump gear
12. Woodruff key
13. Tachometer pinion
14. Thrust washer
15. Oil tube holder
16. Banjo bolt

17. Banjo connection
18. Gasket
19. O-ring
20. O-ring
21. O-ring
22. Spring
23. O-ring
24. O-ring

1. Adjust engine idle speed as described in Chapter Four.

2. Refer to **Figure 8**. Loosen lock nut "B" on the throttle cable, then turn adjuster "A" to provide 0.08 to 0.12 inch (2 to 3 millimeters) play in the throttle cable.

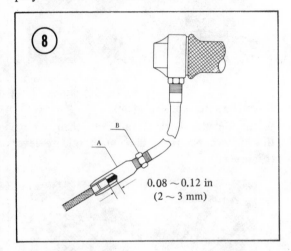

3. Refer to **Figure 9**. Loosen pump cable lock nut "F", then turn adjuster "E" to provide some slack in the cable.

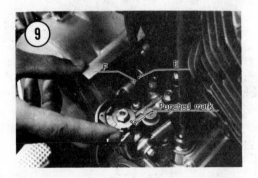

4. There are punched marks on the pump control lever and lever stopper. With these marks aligned, adjust play in the cable to zero with cable adjuster "E".

5. Tighten lock nut "F".

Bleeding the Oil Pump

Air will enter the oil pump whenever the oil tank runs dry or the pump has been disconnected. Any air in the pump or lines will cause an irregular flow of oil, resulting in lack of lubrication. After such an occurrence, the pump must be bled.

1. Loosen the banjo bolt at the oil pump inlet, and force oil into the inlet tube until there are no bubbles. Replace the banjo fitting.

2. Run the engine at approximately 2,000 rpm. *The fuel tank must contain a 15 to 1 fuel/oil mixture.*

3. Pull the pump control lever to the full open position, and hold it until there are no more air bubbles in the outlet tube.

If air bubbles continue to appear in the outlet, check all fittings and connections.

PREPARATION FOR ENGINE DISASSEMBLY

1. Thoroughly clean the engine exterior of dirt, oil, and foreign material, using one of the cleaners formulated for the purpose.

2. Be sure that you have the proper tools for the job. See the general information in Chapter One.

3. As you remove parts from the engine, place them in trays in order of their disassembly. Doing so will make reassembly faster and easier, and will ensure correct installation of all engine parts.

4. Note that the disassembly procedures vary slightly between the different models. Be sure to read the steps carefully and follow those which apply to your engine.

ENGINE REMOVAL

The procedure for removing the engine is generally similar for all models. The following steps are set forth as a guide:

1. If the engine runs, start it and let it run for a few minutes to warm the oil. Then remove the drain plug and drain the transmission oil.

2. Turn the fuel petcock off. Disconnect the fuel lines at the carburetors.

3. Remove the exhaust pipes at the cylinders and the muffler attaching bolts. The mufflers and exhaust pipes may then be removed together (**Figure 10**).

4. Remove the left side cover, then the air cleaner (**Figure 11**).

5. Remove the carburetor cover from each side of the engine, remove the fuel lines, then remove the carburetors (**Figure 12**).

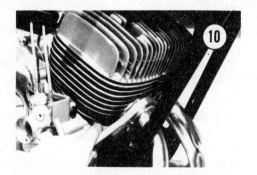

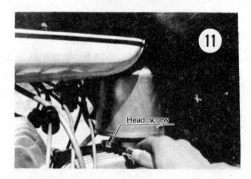

then remove the oil inlet tube. Be sure to plug the tube to prevent loss of oil.

9. Slacken the outer clutch cable, then remove the inner cable from the clutch release lever (**Figure 15**).

6. Remove the attaching screw, then the tachometer cable (**Figure 13**).

10. Remove the front chain cover if necessary, then remove the master link to remove the drive chain. It may be necessary to rotate the rear wheel to position the master link for convenient removal. Upon installation, be sure to position the master link clip as shown in **Figure 16**.

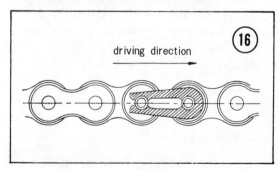

driving direction

7. Remove the oil pump cable from the pump control lever (**Figure 14**).

8. Remove the banjo bolt from the oil pump,

11. Remove the wiring from the alternator.

12. Remove the wires from the spark plugs (**Figure 17**).

13. Remove the engine mounting bolts.

14. Straddle the machine and remove the engine from the frame.

15. Reverse the removal procedure to install the engine. Be sure to check the following items before you start the engine:

 a. Oil supply
 b. Transmission oil level
 c. Clutch adjustment
 d. Oil pump and throttle cables
 e. Drive chain adjustment
 f. Engine mounting bolts
 g. Ignition timing

CYLINDERS AND CYLINDER HEADS

Figure 18 (next page) is a typical exploded view of the cylinders and heads used on twin-cylinder models. The cylinders are made from lightweight aluminum alloy, with cast iron sleeves.

Cylinder Head Removal and Replacement

Remove the special nuts from the cylinder heads, then remove the cylinder heads and gaskets as shown in **Figure 19**. Be sure to use new gaskets upon reassembly. Torque the nuts to approximately 18 foot-pounds (2.5 kg-m).

Gasket

Removing Carbon Deposits

Carbon deposits in the combustion chamber result in an increase in compression ratio and can cause preignition, overheating, and excessive fuel consumption. To remove these deposits, scrape them off with the rounded end of a hacksaw blade or a screwdriver, as shown in **Figure 20**. Be careful that you do not damage the gasket surface.

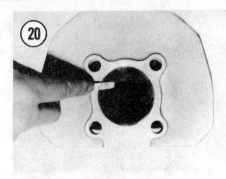

Cylinder Removal

With the cylinder head removed, tap the cylinder around the exhaust port with a plastic mallet, then pull it away from the crankcase. Stuff clean rags into the crankcase openings to prevent entry of any foreign material.

Cylinder Inspection

Measure cylinder wall wear at the 3 locations shown in **Figure 21** with a cylinder gauge or inside micrometer, as shown in **Figure 22**.

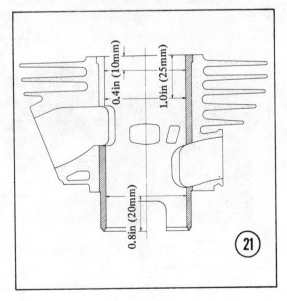

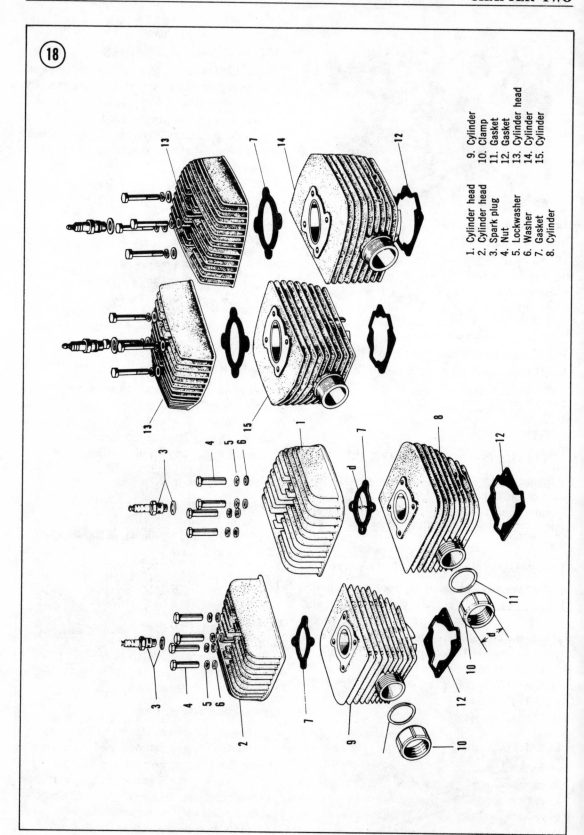

18

1. Cylinder head
2. Cylinder head
3. Spark plug
4. Nut
5. Lockwasher
6. Washer
7. Gasket
8. Cylinder
9. Cylinder
10. Clamp
11. Gasket
12. Gasket
13. Cylinder head
14. Cylinder
15. Cylinder

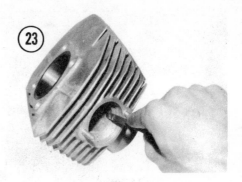

Position the instrument parallel and then at right angles to the crankshaft at each depth. If any measurement exceeds 0.006 inch (0.15 millimeter) over the standard value, or if the difference between any two measurements exceeds 0.002 inch (0.05 millimeter) rebore and hone the cylinder to the next oversize, or replace the cylinder. Pistons are available in oversizes of 0.02 inch (0.50 millimeter) and 0.04 inch (1.00 millimeter). After boring and honing, the difference between maximum and minimum diameters must not be more than 0.0004 inch (0.01 millimeter). Standard measurements are listed in the following table.

Model	Standard Dimensions	
	Inches	(Millimeters)
A1 Series	2.09	(53.0)
A7 Series	2.44	(62.0)

Removing Carbon Deposits

Scrape the carbon deposits from around the cylinder exhaust port, as shown in **Figure 23**. The rounded end of a hacksaw blade is a suitable tool for carbon removal.

Cylinder Installation

Be sure that each piston ring end gap is aligned with the locating pin in the ring groove. Lubricate the piston and cylinder, then insert the piston into the lower end of the cylinder. It will be necessary to compress each piston ring

as it goes into the cylinder. Always use a new cylinder base gasket upon reassembly.

PISTON, PISTON PIN, AND PISTON RINGS

Piston Pin Removal

Remove the clips at each end of the piston pin with needle nose pliers (**Figure 24**). Then press out the piston pin with the piston pin removal tool, as shown in **Figure 25**.

Circlip

Special tool

Piston Ring Replacement

Remove the piston rings by spreading the top ring with a thumb on each end, as shown in **Figure 26**. Then remove the ring from the top of the piston. Repeat the procedure for the remaining ring or rings. The expander rings used on some models may be removed easily by prying the ends apart with a narrow screwdriver.

Measure each ring for wear as shown in **Figure 27**. Insert the ring 0.2 inch (5 millimeters) into the cylinder, then measure the ring gap with a feeler gauge. To ensure that the ring is squarely in the cylinder, push it into position with the head of the piston. The standard gap for all models is 0.008 to 0.012 inch (0.2 to 0.3 millimeter). If the gap exceeds 0.031 inch (0.8 millimeter), replace the rings.

Scrape the carbon from the head of the piston (**Figure 28**). Then clean all carbon and gum from the piston ring grooves (**Figure 29**), using a broken piston ring or a ring groove cleaning tool. Any deposits left in the grooves will cause the rings to stick, thereby causing gas blowby and loss of power.

To check the fit of the piston ring in its groove,

slip the outer surface of the ring into the groove next to the locating pin, then roll the ring completely around the piston. If any binding occurs, determine and correct the cause before proceeding.

When you replace the rings, install the lower one first. Be sure that any printing on the ring is toward the top of the piston. Spread the rings carefully with your thumbs, just enough to slip them over the piston. Align the end gaps with the locating pin in each ring groove. Note that upper and lower rings may be distinguished by color; the upper ring is chrome plated and therefore lighter.

Piston Clearance

Piston clearance (**Figure 30**) is the difference between the maximum piston diameter and the minimum cylinder diameter. Measure the outside diameter of the piston skirt (**Figure 31**) at right angles to the piston pin. The measurement should be made 0.2 inch (5 millimeters) from the bottom of the piston. Proper piston clearances are listed in the following table.

Model	Piston Clearance	
	Inch	(Millimeter)
A1 Series	0.0015	(0.037)
A7 Series	0.0032	(0.081)

A piston showing signs of seizure will result in noise, loss of power, and damage to the cylinder wall. If such a piston is reused without correction, another seizure will develop. To correct this condition, lightly smooth the affected area with No. 400 emery paper or a fine oilstone (**Figure 32**). Replace the piston if it is deeply scratched.

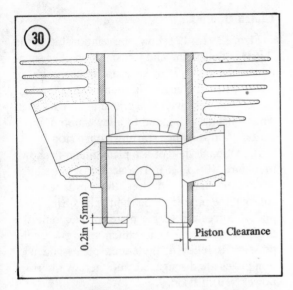

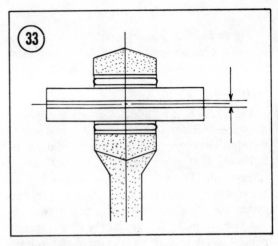

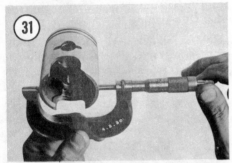

Piston Installation

Install the piston with the arrow mark (**Figure 34**) pointing toward the front of the machine. This is important because the hole for the piston pin is offset slightly (see **Figure 35**) to prevent piston slap.

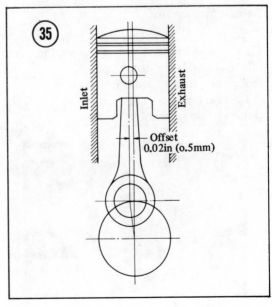

Small End Bearing

Assemble the piston pin, needle bearing, and connecting rod. Measure the radial play, as shown in **Figure 33**. Replace the bearing and/or the piston pin if clearance is over the service limit, or if there are scratches on the piston pin. Standard clearance for all models is 0.00012 to 0.00086 inch (0.003 to 0.022 millimeter). The service limit for all models is 0.004 inch (0.10 millimeter).

CLUTCH

Figure 36 (facing page) is an exploded view of a typical clutch mechanism. Refer to this illustration during clutch service operations.

Operation

Figure 37 is a sectional view of the release mechanism. Refer to this illustration, and also to the clutch exploded view, Figure 36, during the following discussion. The three steel balls in the release ball (2) normally rest in depressions in the clutch release plate (19). As the rider operates the clutch lever on the handlebar, the clutch cable pulls the arm on the clutch release plate, causing it to rotate. As the clutch release plate rotates, the balls are forced out of the depressions. The balls then force the release plate and cam plate (22) apart. The dowel (18) then moves the pusher (12) to release the clutch.

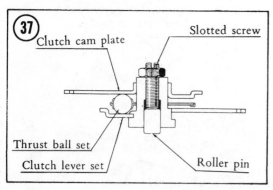

Figure 37 labels: Clutch cam plate · Slotted screw · Thrust ball set · Clutch lever set · Roller pin

Release Mechanism

To remove the release mechanism, refer to **Figure 38**. Remove the three screws, then take off the assembly. Inspect all parts carefully, and replace any that are worn or damaged.

Reverse the removal procedure to install the clutch release mechanism.

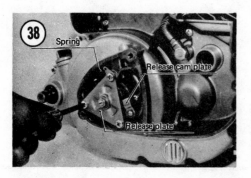

Figure 38 labels: Spring · Release cam plate · Release plate

Clutch Operation

Figure 39 (p. 17) shows the relationship of the clutch to the engine and transmission. The function of the clutch is to interrupt transmission of power when the engine is running and the machine is at rest with the transmission in gear, when shifting gears, and to allow smooth application of power when starting from a stop.

A sectional view of a typical clutch is shown in **Figure 40** (p. 18). The action of the clutch release mechanism moves the push rod and spring plate pusher to the right. The spring plate pusher forces the spring plate to overcome the pressure exerted by the clutch springs. As the pressure is relieved, the clutch plates and friction plates are disengaged, and thereby interrupt power transmission.

Clutch Disassembly

1. Hold the clutch in position and remove the nut (**Figure 41**). Then remove the lockwasher and thrust washer.

Figure 41 labels: Special tool

2. Remove the clutch as an assembly as shown in **Figure 42**.

3. Remove the bushing and thrust washer.

4. Remove the six screws, then the spring plate, clutch plates, and friction plates (**Figure 43**). Note the position of the return rubbers.

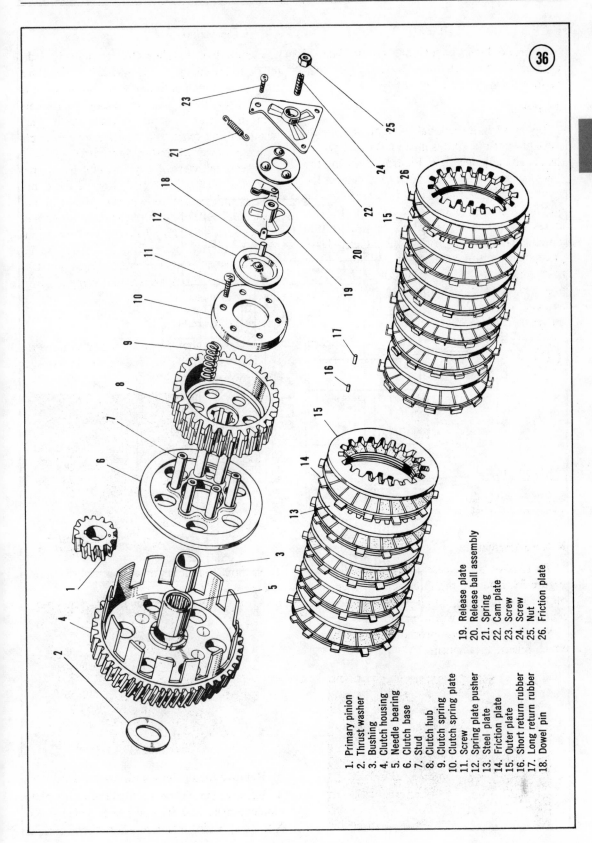

1. Primary pinion
2. Thrust washer
3. Bushing
4. Clutch housing
5. Needle bearing
6. Clutch base
7. Stud
8. Clutch hub
9. Clutch spring
10. Clutch spring plate
11. Screw
12. Spring plate pusher
13. Steel plate
14. Friction plate
15. Outer plate
16. Short return rubber
17. Long return rubber
18. Dowel pin
19. Release plate
20. Release ball assembly
21. Spring
22. Cam plate
23. Screw
24. Screw
25. Nut
26. Friction plate

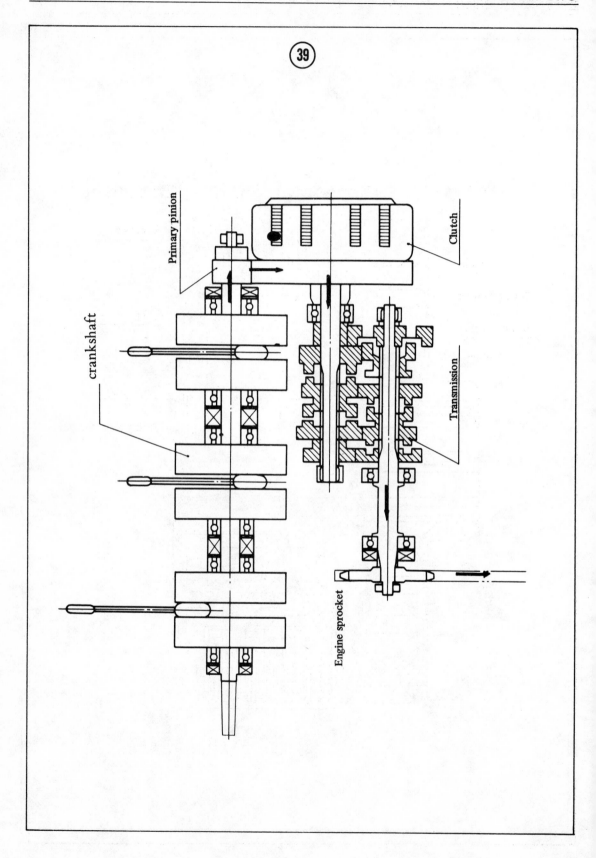

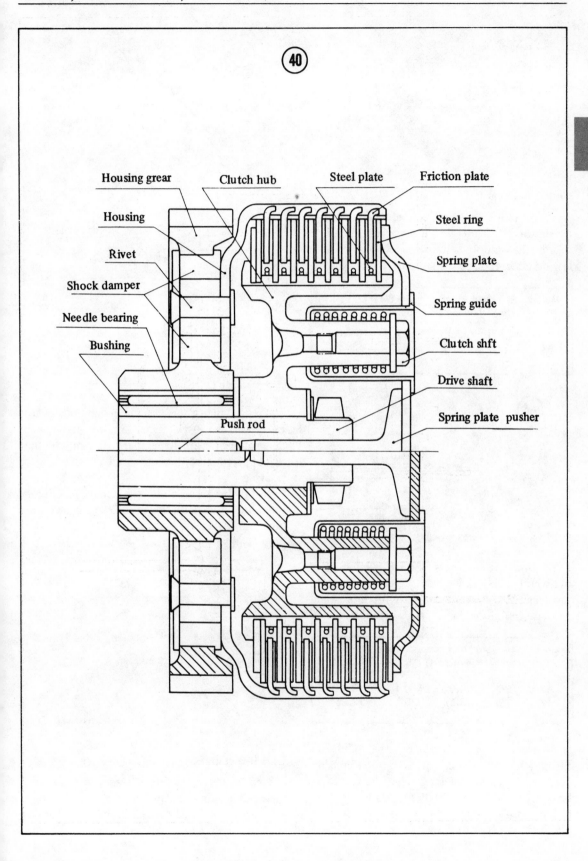

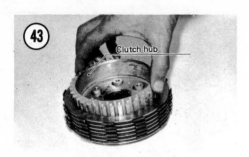

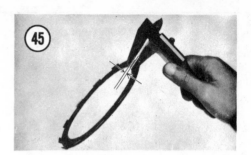

Clutch Inspection

Measure the free length of each clutch spring, as shown in **Figure 44**. If the free length is shorter than the wear limit specified in the following table, replace the spring.

Model	Standard Length		Wear Limit	
	Inches	(Millimeters)	Inches	(Millimeters)
A1	1.18	(29.5)	1.10	(28.0)
A7	1.20	(30.0)	1.13	(28.5)

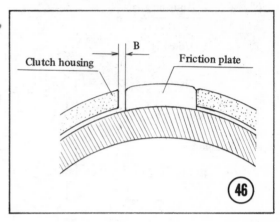

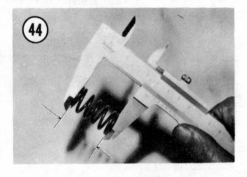

Measure the thickness of each friction plate at several places, as shown in **Figure 45**. Replace any plate that is worn unevenly, or more than the wear limit listed in the following table.

Model	Standard Thickness		Wear Limit	
	Inch	(Millimeters)	Inch	(Millimeters)
A1	0.16	(4.0)	0.14	(3.65)
A7	0.12	(3.1)	0.11	(2.85)

Measure the gap (**B**) between the splines on the clutch friction discs and the clutch housing (**Figure 46**), using a feeler gauge. The gap must be 0.002 to 0.012 inch (0.05 to 0.03 millimeter) to prevent noisy operation. Replace the friction plates if the gap is too large.

Check the gear teeth on the clutch housing for burrs, nicks, or damage. Smooth any such defects with an oilstone. If the oilstone doesn't smooth out the damage, replace the clutch housing.

Insert the bushing into the needle bearing in the clutch housing (**Figure 47**). Replace the bushing if there is noticeable play. Excessive play results in gear noise.

Clutch Installation

Reverse the applicable disassembly procedure to assemble and install the clutch. Note that there are three thrust washers in the clutch. Make sure that they are installed correctly to ensure proper clutch operation. Refer to the exploded view (Figure 36). Be sure to position the long and short return rubbers correctly (**Figure 48**). Be sure that timing marks on the primary gear, clutch gear, and alternator gear are aligned (**Figure 49**).

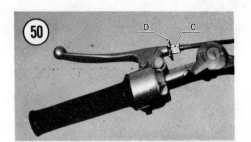

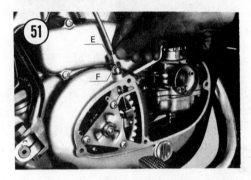

Clutch Adjustment

Refer to **Figures 50 and 51**, then proceed as follows:

1. Loosen lock nuts "D" and "F".

2. Rotate adjustment nuts "C" and "E" until the clutch cable inner wire is completely free.

3. Loosen lock nut "B", as shown in **Figure 52**. Loosen screw "A" until it turns freely. Then turn screw "A" in until the clutch begins to release. Turning torque will increase at this point.

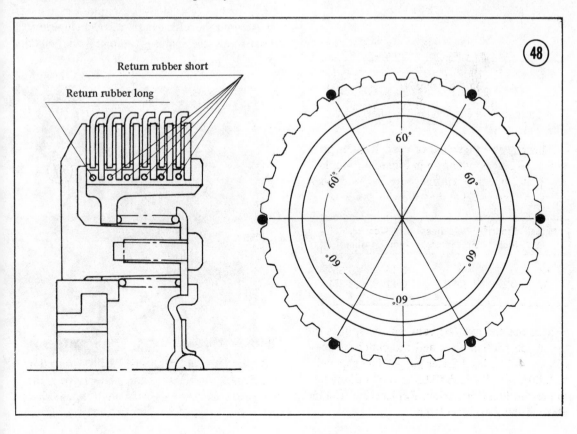

Return rubber short

Return rubber long

60°
60°
60°
60°
60°
.09

4. Back screw "A" out one-quarter to one-half turn, then tighten lock nut "B" securely.

5. Adjust free play in the clutch lever to 0.016 inch (4 millimeters) with cable adjuster "E", as shown in **Figure 53**.

6. Tighten lock nuts "D" and "F".

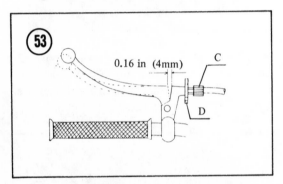

PRIMARY REDUCTION GEARS

Figure 54 illustrates the primary drive on these machines.

Disassembly

1. Straighten the tab on the lockwasher with a chisel.

2. Hold the clutch, then remove the nut (**Figure 55**).

Inspection

Check the gear teeth for burrs, nicks, or scratches. If any small defects are found, smooth the gear teeth with an oilstone. Replace the gear if the oilstone doesn't clean up the defects.

Installation

Reverse the disassembly procedure to replace the gears. Use a new lockwasher upon assembly. Don't forget to bend the tab on the lockwasher.

LEFT ENGINE COVER

Removal

1. Remove the left carburetor cover (**Figure 56**).

2. Remove the banjo bolt and oil tubes from the oil pump, then the pump itself (**Figure 57**).

3. Remove the screws which attach the rotary valve cover cap (**Figure 58**), then the tachometer pinion.

4. Remove the tachometer pinion and oil pump gear (**Figure 59**). Then remove the oil pump pinion.

Inspection

Check the oil seal in the tachometer bushing. If the seal is worn or damaged, replace it.

Installation

Reverse the disassembly procedure to install the left engine cover. Note that the convex end of the oil pump shaft fits into the concave shaft end of the oil pump gear. Be sure to tighten the screws evenly.

ENGINE SPROCKET

The engine sprocket is subject to wear and abrasion from sand and dust, which tend to collect on the sprocket. To minimize wear, the sprocket (**Figure 60**) is made from abrasion resistant steel.

Removal

1. Straighten the tab on the lockwasher, using a small hammer and a chisel (**Figure 61**).

2. Hold the sprocket in position (**Figure 62**), then remove the sprocket nut and sprocket.

Inspection

A worn sprocket results in excessive chain noise, and will shorten the life of the chain. **Figure 63** compares worn and serviceable sprockets. Measure the root diameter, as shown in **Figure 64**. Replace the sprocket if it shows any defects, or if the root diameter is less than specified in the following table.

Sprocket	Standard Dimension		Wear Limit	
	Inches	(Millimeters)	Inches	(Millimeters)
15 teeth	2.60	(65.8)	2.55	(65.0)
16 teeth	2.80	(71.2)	2.75	(70.4)

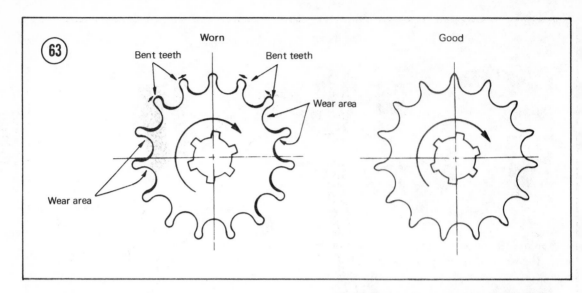

Worn   Good

Bent teeth   Bent teeth

Wear area

Wear area

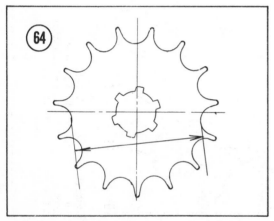

Generator cover

Installation

Reverse the removal procedure to install the sprocket. Use a new lockwasher and be sure to bend up the tab.

ALTERNATOR

Removal

1. Remove the attaching nut, then pull out the alternator drive gear.
2. Remove the cover (**Figure 65**), then remove the alternator.

Inspection and Installation

Refer to Chapter Three for inspection, repair, and installation procedures for the alternator. Be sure that the timing marks on the gears are aligned (**Figure 66**).

GEARSHIFT MECHANISM

Figure 67 is an exploded view of the shifter. **Figure 68** illustrates shifter operation. As the rider presses the gearshift pedal, the shaft turns, and moves the change lever. The change lever meshes with pins on the shift drum (part of the transmission assembly). Therefore, as the pedal is moved, the shift drum rotates. Grooves on the shift drum cause shift forks in the transmission

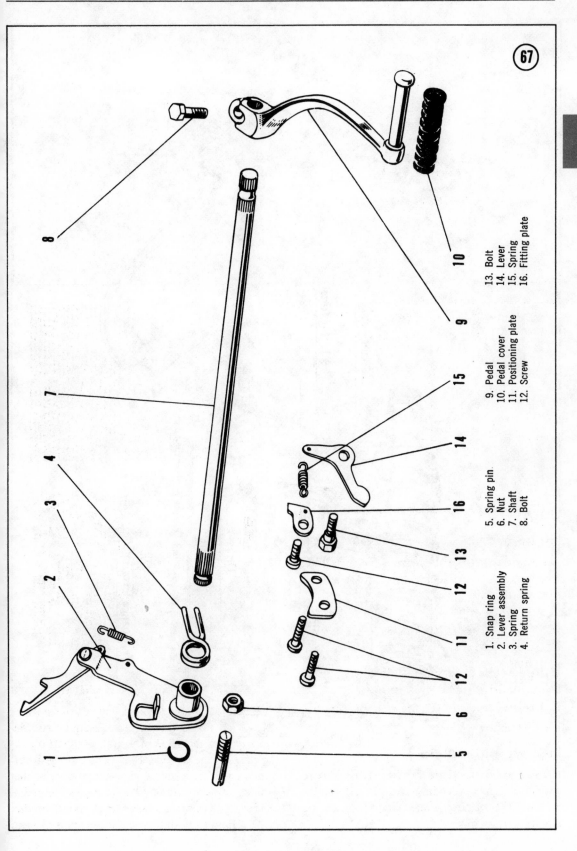

67

1. Snap ring
2. Lever assembly
3. Spring
4. Return spring
5. Spring pin
6. Nut
7. Shaft
8. Bolt
9. Pedal
10. Pedal cover
11. Positioning plate
12. Screw
13. Bolt
14. Lever
15. Spring
16. Fitting plate

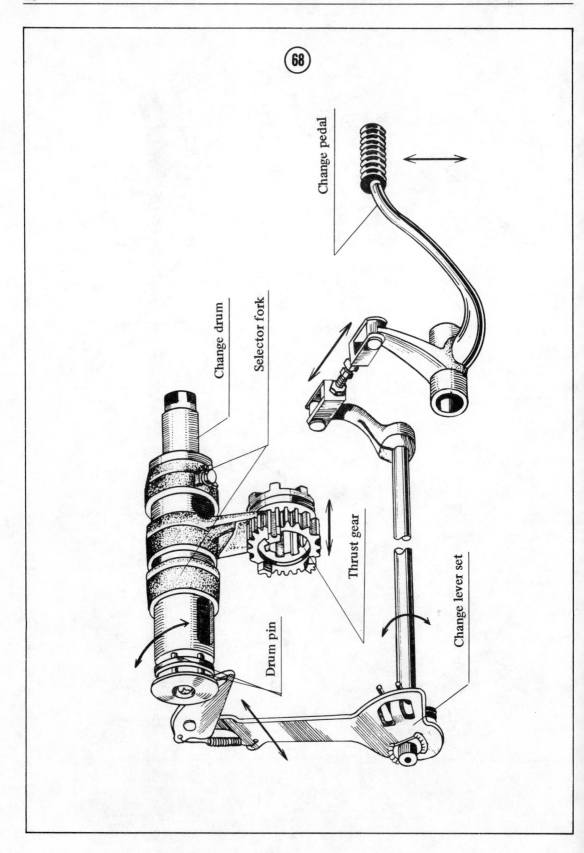

to move, and thereby select the various gear ratios.

Set levers are also meshed with the pins on the change drum. They keep the drum in position after each step of rotation of the drum.

Removal

1. Disengage the set levers and change lever from the change drum pins (**Figure 69**).

2. Remove the hex bolt from the set lever (**Figure 70**).
3. Pull out the change lever and shaft as a unit.

Inspection

Check the return spring tension (**Figure 71**). Replace the spring if it is weak or cracked. Inspect the set lever spring for cracks or weakness.

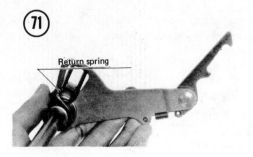

Be sure that the return spring set pin is not loose. If this pin is loose, missed shifts will result. Be sure that the lock nut is tight.

Installation

Reverse the removal procedure to install the shift mechanism. Be sure that each spring is installed correctly.

ROTARY VALVE

The rotary valve system consists of the crankshaft, disc valves, crankcase, and valve covers. **Figure 72** (next page) illustrates the valve mechanism. The valves are made from hardened phenol resin, with steel centers.

The valves float back and forth slightly on the crankshaft. This floating action permits the valve to seat against the O-ring on the valve cover, and thereby seal the crankcase during the down stroke of the piston.

Removal

1. Remove the valve cover retaining screws, then pull off the valve cover (**Figure 73**).

2. Slide the valve disc (**Figure 74**) from the shaft.

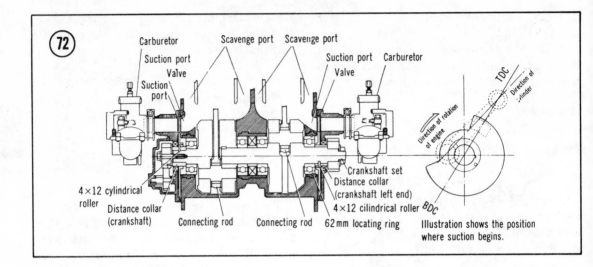

3. Remove the spacer and O-ring from the crankshaft.

4. Remove the dowel pin.

Inspection

Figure 75 illustrates the valve cover. Examine the oil seal for scratches, lip deformation, or other damage. Check for any damage to the O-ring. Replace the valve cover in the event of deep scratches, or if it is worn to a depth of 0.16 inch (4.0 millimeters) as shown in **Figure 76**. Standard valve cover depth is 0.14 inch (3.5 millimeters).

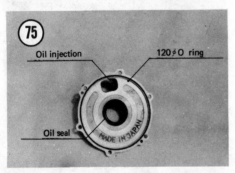

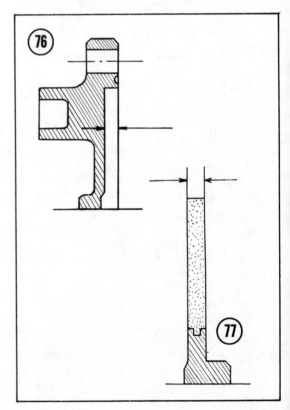

Measure the thickness of the valve disc, as shown in **Figure 77**. Replace the disc if it is worn beyond the wear limit, or if there are any scratches or damage on its surface. Standard thickness is 0.14 inch (3.5 millimeters).

Installation

Reverse the removal procedure to install the valve. Soak the disc in two-stroke oil before installation. Be sure that the O-ring is installed correctly in the valve cover.

CRANKCASE

Figure 78 (page 30) is an exploded view of the crankcase. The crankcase supports the crankshaft, transmission, and kickstarter, as shown in **Figure 79**.

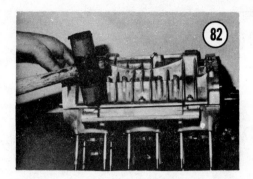

Lubricating oil passages are machined in the crankcase. Be very careful that these passages don't become clogged with dirt when you work on the crankcase.

Disassembly

1. Remove the oil reservoir at the output shaft (**Figure 80**).

2. Invert the crankcase, then remove the nuts from the bottom side (**Figure 81**).

3. With the crankcase still inverted, tap the crankcase and shifter shaft boss with a plastic mallet (**Figure 82**) to separate the two halves.

4. Remove the crankshaft, transmission, and kickstarter assemblies.

Inspection

Check each lubrication passage. If any is found to be clogged, blow it out with compressed air. Check the transmission breather hole. Oil leakage will result if this hole is clogged. Examine the mating surfaces of the crankcase halves. Any nicks or scratches will result in oil leakage.

Reassembly

1. Install the internal parts into the upper crankcase. **Figure 83** shows the parts installed.

2. Clean the mating surfaces carefully with solvent.

3. Apply gasket cement to the mating surfaces. Follow the application instructions furnished by the manufacturer.

4. Place the lower crankcase half into position, then tighten the nuts (**Figure 84**) as specified.

Nut Size	Torque
6 millimeters	7.5 ft-lbs (1 kg-m)
8 millimeters	15 ft-lbs (2 kg-m)
10 millimeters	25 ft-lbs (3.5 kg-m)

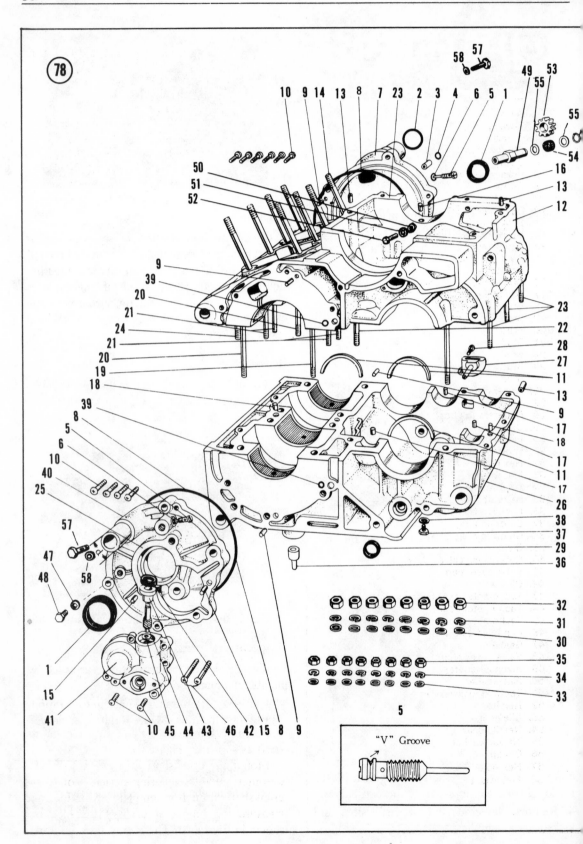

"V" Groove

5

1. Oil seal
2. O-ring
3. Dowel pin
4. O-ring
5. Oil injection nozzle
6. O-ring
7. Rotary disc valve cover
8. O-ring
9. Dowel pin
10. Pan head screw
11. Setting ring
12. Upper crankcase half
13. Dowel pin
14. Stud
15. Dowel pin
16. Dowel pin
17. Dowel pin
18. Dowel pin
19. Stud
20. Stud
21. Stud
22. Stud
23. Stud
24. Stud
26. Lower crankcase half
27. Oil receiver
28. Countersunk head screw
29. Oil seal
30. Flat washer
31. Lockwasher
32. Hex nut
33. Flat washer
34. Lockwasher
35. Hex nut
36. Fuel overflow tube
37. Oil drain plug
38. Oil drain plug gasket
39. O-ring
40. Rotary disc valve cover
41. Valve cover cap
42. Oil seal
43. Tachometer gear bushing
44. Tachometer gear
45. Tachometer gear thrust washer
46. Pan head screw
47. Gasket
48. Valve cover plug
49. Idle gear shaft
50. Flat washer
51. Toothed lockwasher
52. Hex bolt
53. Idle gear
54. Needle bearing
55. Thrust washer
56. Circlip
57. Hex bolt
58. Flat washer

CRANKSHAFT

The crankshaft operates under conditions of high stress. Dimensional tolerances are critical. It is necessary to locate and correct defects in the crankshaft to prevent more serious trouble later. **Figure 85** (next page) illustrates the crankshaft assembly and related components.

Removal

To remove the crankshaft, tap each end lightly with a plastic mallet, as shown in **Figure 86**.

Inspection

The crankshaft is serviced as a complete assembly; it cannot be disassembled. If the following checks reveal any defects, the crankshaft must be replaced. The right and left oil seals are replaceable, however. Pull the seals from the shaft as shown in **Figure 87**.

Mount the crankshaft in a lathe, V-blocks, or other suitable centering device. Rotate the crankshaft through a complete revolution, and measure the runout at each of the locations shown in **Figure 88**. The runout limit on a new

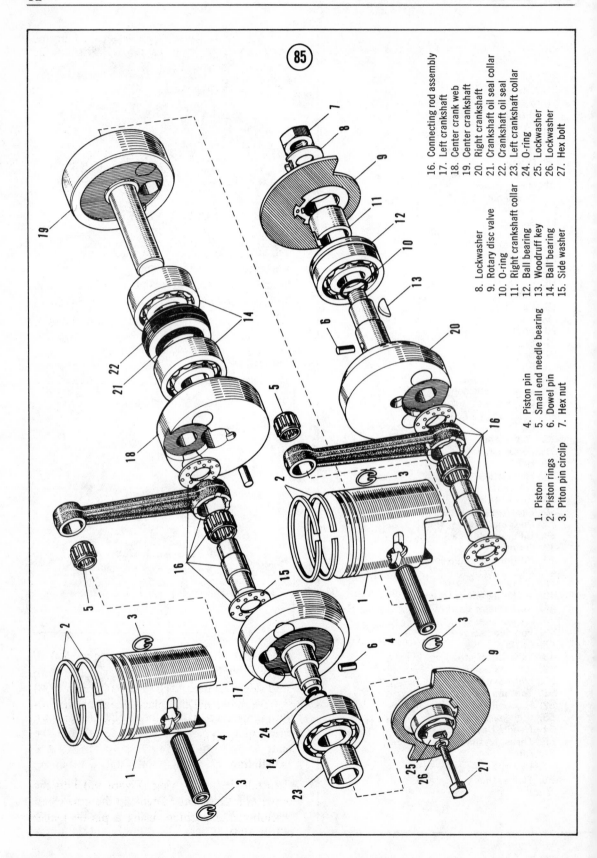

85

1. Piston
2. Piston rings
3. Piton pin circlip
4. Piston pin
5. Small end needle bearing
6. Dowel pin
7. Hex nut
8. Lockwasher
9. Rotary disc valve
10. O-ring
11. Right crankshaft collar
12. Ball bearing
13. Woodruff key
14. Ball bearing
15. Side washer
16. Connecting rod assembly
17. Left crankshaft
18. Center crank web
19. Center crankshaft
20. Right crankshaft
21. Crankshaft oil seal collar
22. Crankshaft oil seal
23. Left crankshaft collar
24. O-ring
25. Lockwasher
26. Lockwasher
27. Hex bolt

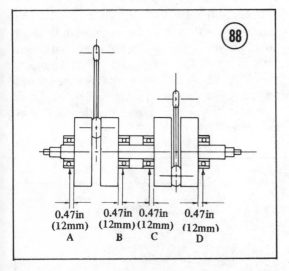

crankshaft assembly should not exceed 0.0008 inch (0.102 millimeter) at any measurement location. Replace the crankshaft assembly if any measurement exceeds 0.0024 inch (0.06 millimeter).

Clean the main bearings (**Figure 89**) thoroughly, then lubricate lightly and spin them to determine their condition. Listen carefully for any unusual noises as they coast down. Rotate them slowly by hand to check for any binding or roughness. Be sure to lubricate the bearings before you reinstall the crankshaft.

Check the oil seals (**Figure 90**) for damage or evidence of leakage. Primary compression leakage will occur if the oil seals leak, thereby causing poor performance.

Measure the radial clearance (**Figure 91**) of the big end of each connecting rod. Standard clearance is 0.00016 to 0.00047 inch (0.004 to 0.012 millimeter). Replace the crankshaft assembly if side clearance exceeds 0.028 inch (0.05 millimeter).

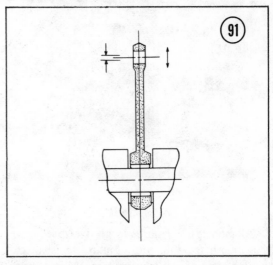

Measure the side clearance (**Figure 92**) of each connecting rod, using a feeler gauge. Standard side clearance is 0.016 to 0.020 inch (0.40 to 0.50 millimeter). Replace the crankshaft assembly if side clearance exceeds 0.028 inch (0.7 millimeter).

Installation

Install the setting ring (**Figure 93**) into the upper crankcase half. Then tap the crankshaft assembly into position, using a plastic mallet (**Figure 94**).

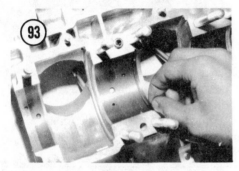

Transmission Operation

Figure 96 (p. 36) is a sectional view of the transmission. Gears D2, D3, 04, and 05 are splined to their shafts. Gear D1 is part of the drive shaft. Gears D4, D5, 01, 02, and 03 are free to rotate on their respective shafts. Gears D3, 04, and 05 are moved left or right along the shafts by the action of the shifter forks.

Consider third gear as an example. Gear 04 is moved to the right by its shift fork. Dog clutches on gears 04 and 03 interlock. The power flow is then from the input shaft, through gear D3, which is splined to the input shaft, then through gear 03, the dog clutch which connects gears 03 and 04, and finally through the splines on gear 04 to the output shaft.

Power flow for each gear position is shown in **Figures 97 through 102**.

Figure	Gear
97	Neutral
98	1st
99	2nd
100	3rd
101	4th
102	5th

Low gear

TRANSMISSION

All models are equipped with five-speed, constant mesh transmissions. **Figure 95** is an exploded view of the transmission. All transmissions are similar in construction and operation. The output shaft is supported by two bearings. The following table lists individual gear ratios within each transmission:

Gear	Ratio
1st	2.50 to 1
2nd	1.53 to 1
3rd	1.13 to 1
4th	0.92 to 1
5th	0.78 to 1

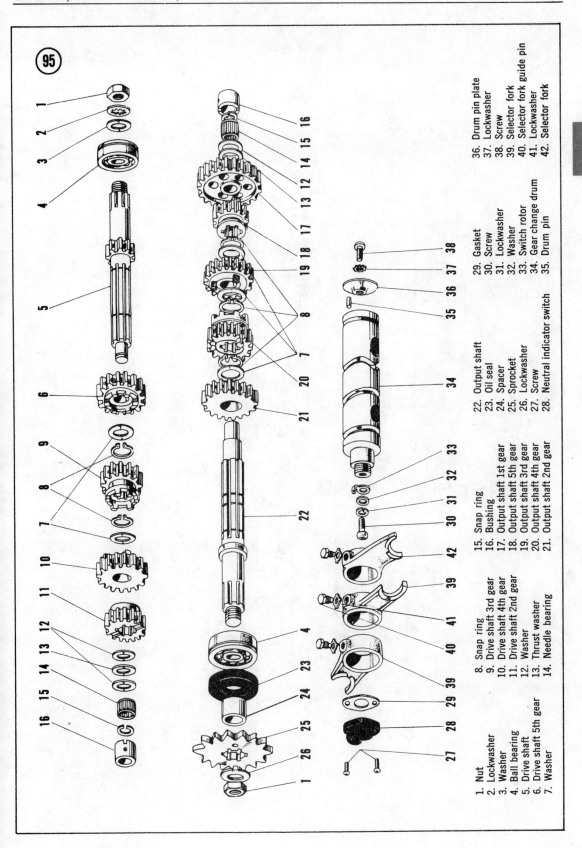

1. Nut
2. Lockwasher
3. Washer
4. Ball bearing
5. Drive shaft
6. Drive shaft 5th gear
7. Washer
8. Snap ring
9. Drive shaft 3rd gear
10. Drive shaft 4th gear
11. Drive shaft 2nd gear
12. Washer
13. Thrust washer
14. Needle bearing
15. Snap ring
16. Bushing
17. Output shaft 1st gear
18. Output shaft 5th gear
19. Output shaft 3rd gear
20. Output shaft 4th gear
21. Output shaft 2nd gear
22. Output shaft
23. Oil seal
24. Spacer
25. Sprocket
26. Lockwasher
27. Screw
28. Neutral indicator switch
29. Gasket
30. Screw
31. Lockwasher
32. Washer
33. Switch rotor
34. Gear change drum
35. Drum pin
36. Drum pin plate
37. Lockwasher
38. Screw
39. Selector fork
40. Selector fork guide pin
41. Lockwasher
42. Selector fork

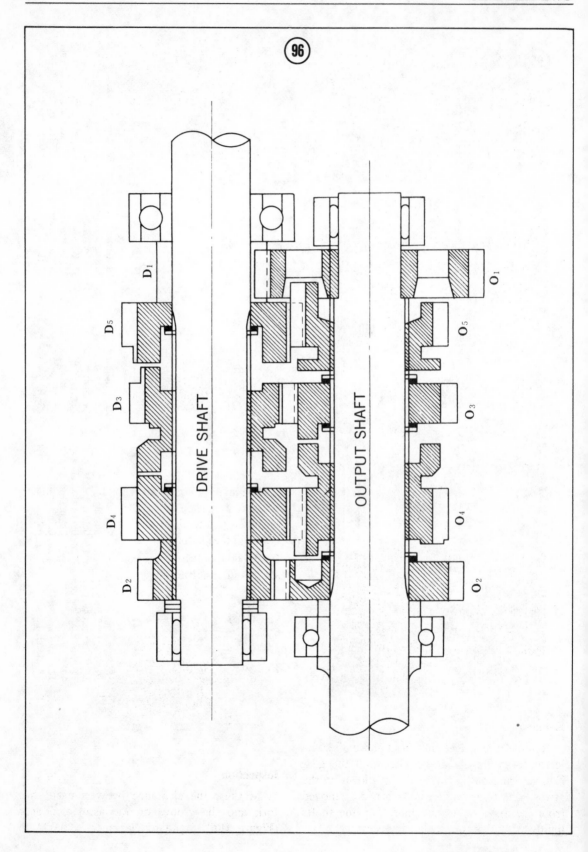

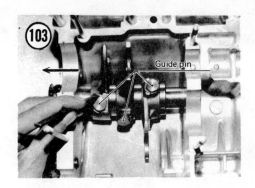

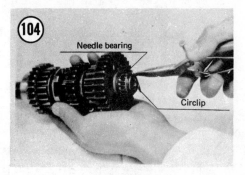

Disassembly

1. Remove the snap rings (**Figure 104**) from the needle bearings.

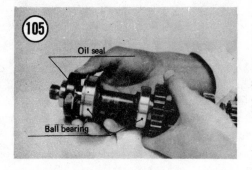

2. Remove each gear individually by removing its associated snap ring and washer. Pay particular attention to the order in which the gears come off the shafts.

3. Pull the ball bearings and oil seals from the shafts (**Figure 105**).

Removal

Remove the guide pins from the shifter selector forks (**Figure 103**). Then pull the gear change drum out in the direction shown by the arrow. The transmission may then be removed from the upper crankcase half. Tap the shafts lightly with a plastic mallet if necessary.

Inspection

1. Measure the clearance between each shift fork and the groove on the associated gear (**Figure 106**). Standard clearance is 0.004 to

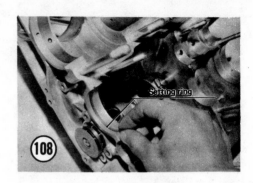

0.01 inch (0.1 to 0.25 millimeter). Replace the gear and/or the fork if clearance exceeds 0.024 inch (0.6 millimeter). Replace the shaft fork if there are any burrs or other damage.

2. Any burrs, pits, or roughness on the gear teeth will cause wear on the mating gear. Replace any gear with such defects. Examine its mating gear carefully and replace it if there is any doubt about its condition. It may be possible to smooth minor burrs with an oilstone.

Reassembly and Installation

To assemble the transmission, reverse the disassembly procedure. Observe the following notes:

1. Install the gear exchange drum (**Figure 107**) into the upper crankcase half first.

2. Be sure the gears are installed correctly on their shafts, and that each snap ring is seated in its groove.

3. Install the setting rings (**Figure 108**) before you install the transmission.

4. Be sure the lockwasher tabs on the shift fork guide pins are bent over.

KICKSTARTER

Figure 109 is an exploded view of the kick-starter mechanism. As the rider presses the kick-starter pedal, the kick shaft rotates clockwise (**Figure 110**). As the kick shaft rotates, the kick pawl spring and kick pawl pin push the kick pawl away from the kick pawl stopper, and into engagement with the internal teeth of the kick gear. After the engine starts, and the kick pedal is released, the kick shaft returns to its original position. At this time, the kick pawl stopper (**Figure 111**) contacts the kick pawl and holds the kick pawl away from the kick gear, thereby releasing the mechanism during normal running.

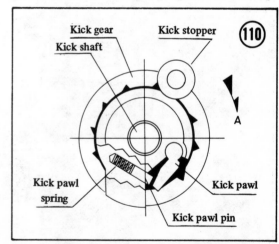

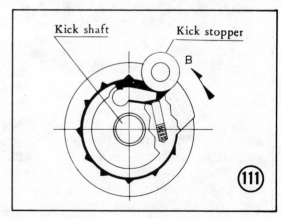

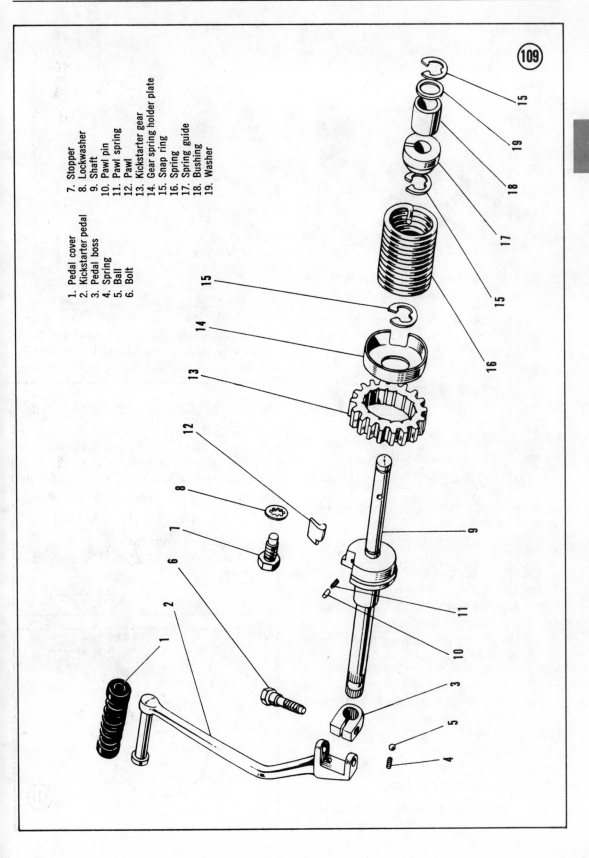

109

1. Pedal cover
2. Kickstarter pedal
3. Pedal boss
4. Spring
5. Ball
6. Bolt
7. Stopper
8. Lockwasher
9. Shaft
10. Pawl pin
11. Pawl spring
12. Pawl
13. Kickstarter gear
14. Gear spring holder plate
15. Snap ring
16. Spring
17. Spring guide
18. Bushing
19. Washer

2

Disassembly

1. Remove the snap ring (**Figure 112**), then pull off the thrust washer, bushing, spring guide, and spring.

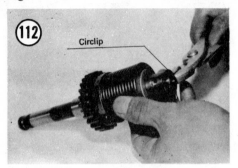

2. Remove the snap ring (**Figure 113**), then remove the kick gear and holder plate.

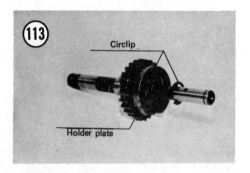

3. Remove the kick pawl, pawl pin, and spring from the kick shaft.

Inspection

1. Check the inner teeth of the kick gear (see **Figure 114**) for wear. If these teeth are worn or rounded, the pawl will slip. Replace the gear if the teeth are worn or damaged.

2. Check for wear on the tip of the kick pawl. Wear results in slippage. Replace the pawl if the tip is worn.

3. Be sure that there is no foreign material in the pawl pin hole. Check for freedom of movement of the pawl pin and pawl spring as shown in **Figure 115**.

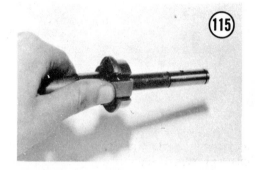

Reassembly and Installation

Reverse the disassembly procedure to assemble the kickstarter. After the crankcase is assembled, install the kick stopper. Rotate the kickstarter pedal downward approximately 150 degrees (**Figure 116**), then install the stopper.

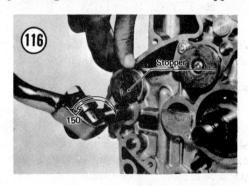

CHAPTER THREE

ELECTRICAL SYSTEM

This chapter discusses operating principles and troubleshooting procedures for the ignition, charging, signal, and lighting systems. Kawasaki twin-cylinder machines are equipped with either a conventional battery ignition system or a capacitor discharge system, which uses no breaker points. All models use alternators as the source of electrical system power.

BATTERY IGNITION SYSTEM

The battery ignition system is used mainly on A1 series machines. This system functions in a manner similar to that of an automobile.

Functional Operation

Figure 1 illustrates the battery ignition system used on these machines. Note that the system is shown for a single cylinder only; all components except the battery, fuse, and ignition switch are duplicated for the other cylinder.

When the breaker points are closed, current flows from the battery through the primary winding of the ignition coil, thereby building a magnetic field around the coil. The breaker cam rotates at crankshaft speed and is so adjusted that the breaker points open as the piston reaches the firing position.

As the points open, the magnetic field collapses. When the magnetic field collapses, a very high voltage is induced (approximately 15,000 volts) in the secondary winding of the ignition coil. This high voltage is sufficient to jump the gap at the spark plug.

The condenser serves primarily to protect the points. Inductance of the ignition coil primarily tends to keep a surge of current flowing through the circuit even after the points have started to open. The condenser stores this surge and thus prevents arcing at the points.

Point Adjustment

Figure 2 illustrates the ignition points on these models. To adjust the points, proceed as follows:

1. Turn the alternator rotor shaft with a wrench until the left-hand breaker points are fully open.

2. Loosen the two clamp screws (D and E) enough so that the stationary contact may be moved.

3. Turn the adjusting screw (B) until a 0.012 to 0.016 inch (0.3 to 0.4 millimeter) feeler gauge just enters the gap between the points.

4. Tighten the two screws (D and E) and recheck the adjustment.

5. Adjust the right-hand points in a similar manner.

6. Be sure to adjust the ignition timing after you adjust the points.

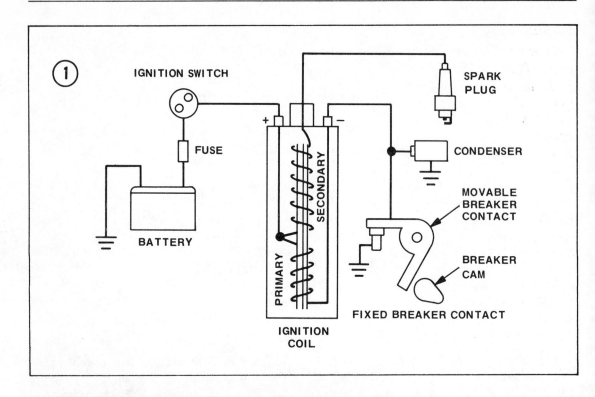

Ignition Timing

To adjust the ignition timing on these models, refer to **Figure 3**. Then proceed as follows:

1. Rotate the engine to align the timing pointer (K) with the painted mark (J). At this point, the crankshaft is 23 degrees before left top dead center.

2. Loosen two clamp screws (L and M) on the base plate.

3. Move the base plate by prying with a screwdriver between the pry points (O and P) until the left-hand points just begin to open. Point opening is most easily determined by disconnecting the spark plug wire and holding it one-quarter inch from the cylinder head with the ignition on. A spark will jump to the cylinder head as the points open.

4. Tighten the two clamp screws (L and M), then recheck the adjustment.

5. After timing is set for the right cylinder, turn the shaft until the red mark aligns with the timing pointer.

6. Loosen two clamp screws (T and U).

7. Insert a screwdriver into the remaining pry point (N). Move the plate until the points for the left cylinder just begin to open.

8. Tighten both clamp screws, then recheck the adjustment.

9. Apply a small quantity of distributor cam lubricant to the felt cam lubricator each time the points are inspected or serviced.

Battery Ignition Troubleshooting

Ignition system problems can be classified as no spark, weak spark, or improperly timed spark. These conditions can affect either or both cylinders of a twin-cylinder engine. The following table on the next page lists common causes and remedies for ignition system malfunctions.

If the problem is no spark at either cylinder, it is almost certainly because current is not reaching either coil. Since the only current path is through the battery connections and the main switch, the defect will be easy to locate.

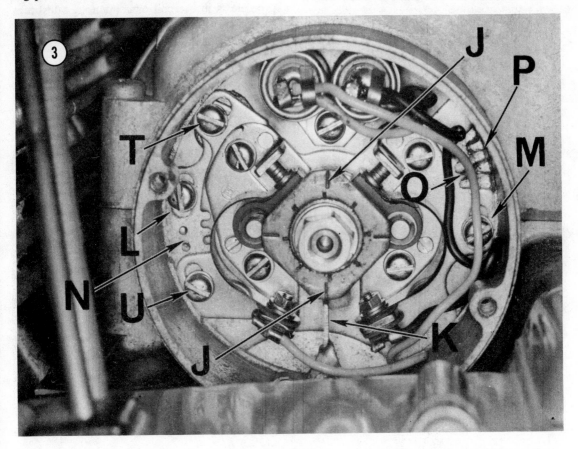

Symptoms	Probable Cause	Remedy
No spark, or weak spark, both cylinders.	Discharged battery	Change battery
	Defective fuse	Replace
	Defective main switch	Replace
	Loose or corroded connections	Clean and tighten
	Broken wire	Repair
No spark or weak spark, on cylinder only.	Incorrect point gap	Reset points. Be sure to readjust ignition timing
	Dirty or oily points	Clean points
	Spark plug lead damaged	Replace wire
	Broken primary wire	Repair wire
	Open winding in coil	Replace coil
	Shorted winding in coil	Replace coil
	Defective Condenser	Replace condenser
Misfires	Dirty spark plug	Clean or replace plug
	Spark plug is too hot	Replace with colder plug
	Spark plug is too cold	Replace with hotter plug
	Spring on ignition points is weak	Replace points, reset timing
	Incorrect timing	Adjust timing

Ignition failures confined to one cylinder are also easy to isolate.

1. Rotate the engine until the points associated with affected cylinder are closed. The points are shown in Figure 2.

2. Disconnect the high voltage lead from the affected spark plug and hold it one-quarter inch away from the cylinder head. Turn on the ignition. With an insulated tool, such as a piece of wood, open the points. A fat, blue-white spark should jump from the spark plug lead to the cylinder head. If the spark is good, clean or replace the spark plug. If there is no spark, or if it is thin, yellowish, or weak, continue with step (3).

3. Connect the leads of a voltmeter to the wire on the points and to a good ground. Turn on the ignition switch. If the meter indicates more than $\frac{1}{8}$ volt, the points are defective. Replace them.

4. Open the points with an insulated tool, such as a piece of wood. The voltmeter should indicate battery voltage. If not, there are three possibilities:

a. shorted points

b. shorted condenser

c. open coil primary circuit

5. Disconnect the condenser and the wire from the points. Connect the ungrounded (positive) voltmeter lead to the wire which was connected to the points. If the voltmeter does not indicate battery voltage, the problem is an open coil primary circuit. Replace the suspected coil with a known good one from the other cylinder. If that coil doesn't work, the problem is in the primary wiring.

6. If the voltmeter indicated battery voltage in step (5), the coil primary circuit is okay. Connect the positive voltmeter lead to the wire which goes from the coil to the points. Block the points open with a calling card or similar piece of cardboard. Connect the negative voltmeter lead to the movable point. If the voltmeter indicates any voltage, the points are shorted and must be replaced.

7. If the foregoing checks are satisfactory, the problem is in the coil or condenser. Substitute each of these separately with a known good one from the other cylinder to determine which is defective.

Spark Plugs

The spark plugs recommended by the factory are usually the most suitable for your machine. Refer to the specifications, Chapter Eight, for the recommended spark plugs for each machine. If your riding conditions are mild, it may be advisable to go to spark plugs one step hotter than normal. Unusually severe riding conditions may require slightly colder plugs.

The proper heat range for the spark plugs is determined by the requirement that the plugs operate hot enough to burn off unwanted deposits, but not so hot that they burn themselves or cause preignition. A spark plug of the correct heat range will show a light tan color on that portion of the insulator within the cylinder after the plug has been in service.

If the insulator appears to be burned or white, the plug is too hot. Possibly the insulator and center electrode will even show evidence of melting. Such plugs should be replaced with colder ones.

Unburned residue such as fluffy black carbon or grimy oil deposits indicate a spark plug that is too cold. The insulator color may range from dark brown to black. Try using hotter plugs if these conditions are found.

Remove and clean the spark plugs approximately every 1,000 miles (1,500 kilometers). After cleaning, inspect them for worn or eroded electrodes. Replace them if there is any doubt about their condition. If the plugs are found to be serviceable, file the center electrodes square, then adjust the gaps by bending the outer electrodes only. Measure the gaps with a round wire spark plug gauge only; a flat gauge will yield an incorrect reading. **Figure 4** illustrates the proper spark plug gap.

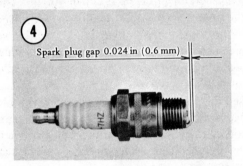

Should you encounter difficulty removing the spark plug, apply penetrating oil to the base of the plug and allow time for the oil to work in. Be sure to clean the seating area on the cylinder head and use a new gasket when you replace the spark plug. Install the plug finger-tight, then tighten it an additional half turn.

Ignition Coil

The ignition coil is a form of transformer which develops the high voltage required to jump the spark plug gap. The only maintenance required is that of keeping the electrical connections clean and tight, and occasionally checking to see that the coil is mounted securely.

If the condition of the coil is doubtful, there are several checks which should be made.

1. Measure the resistance with an ohmmeter between the positive and negative primary terminals. Resistance should measure approximately five ohms. Some coils, however, have a primary resistance of less than one ohm. Com-pare the measurement with that of a known good coil.

2. Measure the resistance between either primary terminal and the secondary high voltage terminal. Resistance should be in the range of 5,000 to 11,000 ohms.

3. Scrape the paint from the coil housing down to bare metal. Set the ohmmeter to its highest range, then measure the insulation resistance between this bare spot and the high voltage terminal. Insulation resistance must be at least 3 megohms (3 million ohms).

4. If these checks don't reveal any defects, but the coil condition is still doubtful, substitute a known good one.

Be sure that you connect the primary wires correctly when you replace the coil.

Condenser

The condenser is a sealed unit that requires no maintenance. Be sure that both connections are clean and tight.

Two tests can be made on the condenser. Measure condenser capacity with a condenser tester. Capacity should be 0.18 to 0.25 microfarad. The other test is insulation resistance, which should not be less than 5 megohms, measured between the condenser pigtail and case.

In the event that no test equipment is available, a quick test of the condenser may be made by connecting the condenser case to the negative terminal of a 12-volt battery, and the positive lead to the positive battery terminal. Allow the condenser to charge for a few seconds, then quickly disconnect the battery and touch the condenser pigtail to the condenser case. If you observe a spark as the pigtail touches the case, you may assume that the condenser is okay.

Arcing between the breaker points is a common symptom of condenser failure.

Ignition Points

There is one set of points for each cylinder. Normal use of the motorcycle causes the points to burn and pit gradually. If the points are not too pitted, they can be dressed with a few strokes of a clean point file. Do not use emery cloth or sandpaper, as particles can remain on the points and cause arcing and burning. If a few strokes of the file don't smooth the points completely, replace them.

Oil or dirt may get on the points, resulting in premature failure. Common causes for this condition are defective crankshaft seals, improper lubrication of the breaker cam, or lack of care when the crankcase cover is removed.

If the point spring is weak, the points will bounce and cause misfiring at high speeds.

Clean and regap the points from time to time. To clean the points, dress them lightly with a point file, then remove all residue with lacquer thinner. Close the points on a piece of clean white paper such as a business card. Continue to pull the card through the closed points until no particles or discoloration remain on the card. Finally, rotate the engine as you observe the points as they open and close. If they do not meet squarely, replace them.

Ignition timing is affected by any change in point gap. Always adjust the timing after you service the points.

CAPACITOR DISCHARGE IGNITION SYSTEM

Some models are equipped with a capacitor discharge ignition system (CDI). This system, unlike battery or magneto ignition systems, uses no breaker points or other moving parts. Special surface-gap spark plugs are used with this system. Because of the extremely fast rise time of the high voltage, spark plug fouling is minimized.

CDI Operation

Figure 5 is a schematic diagram of the capacitor discharge system. Battery voltage is converted to alternating current, then stepped up, and rectified into high voltage direct current in the AC to DC converter. This current charges the capacitor (condendser) in the condenser discharge circuit.

A small magnet attached to, and rotating with, the alternator shaft generates a pulse in the signal pickup coil in the alternator. This pulse is amplified, then shaped, and used to trigger the thyristor. When the thyristor is triggered, it conducts, and thereby provides a discharge path for the capacitor.

The capacitor discharges very quickly into the primary circuit of the ignition coil, where it is stepped up to approximately 20,000 volts.

Ignition Timing

Figure 6 shows the two signal pickup coils in the alternator. Refer to the illustration and proceed as follows:

1. Loosen the clamp screws (1, 2, 3, and 4) on the pickup coils and adjust the coils so that there is a gap of 0.016 to 0.024 inch (0.4 to 0.6 millimeter) between each coil and the signal generator rotor. Be sure to retighten the screws.

2. Rotate the engine so that the center of the pointer aligns with the stamped line on the signal generator rotor. Be sure that you don't align the pointer with the line on either projection on the signal generator rotor.

3. Loosen the clamp screws (5, 8, and 9) on the signal generator plate.

4. Insert a screwdriver between the screw (9) and the projection on the signal generator plate. Move the plate so that the stamped line on one rotor projection aligns with the line on pickup coil number 2. Don't forget to tighten the clamp screws (5, 8, and 9).

5. Turn the rotor counterclockwise 90 degrees, so that the line on the rotor projection aligns with the center of the pointer.

6. Loosen the clamp screws (6 and 7) on the primary pickup coil.

7. Adjust the primary pickup so that the stamped line on the pickup coil aligns with the stamped line on the rotor. Then tighten the clamp screws (6 and 7).

If the alternator is removed or disassembled, the position of the pointer will change. It will then be necessary to adjust the pointer position.

1. Mount the dial gauge in the spark plug hole in the right cylinder head.

2. Slowly rotate the engine until the piston is at top dead center, as indicated by the dial gauge. Zero the dial gauge.

3. Rotate the engine backward to lower the piston approximately one-quarter inch (6 millimeters).

4. Very slowly rotate the engine in its normal direction until the dial gauge indicates that the

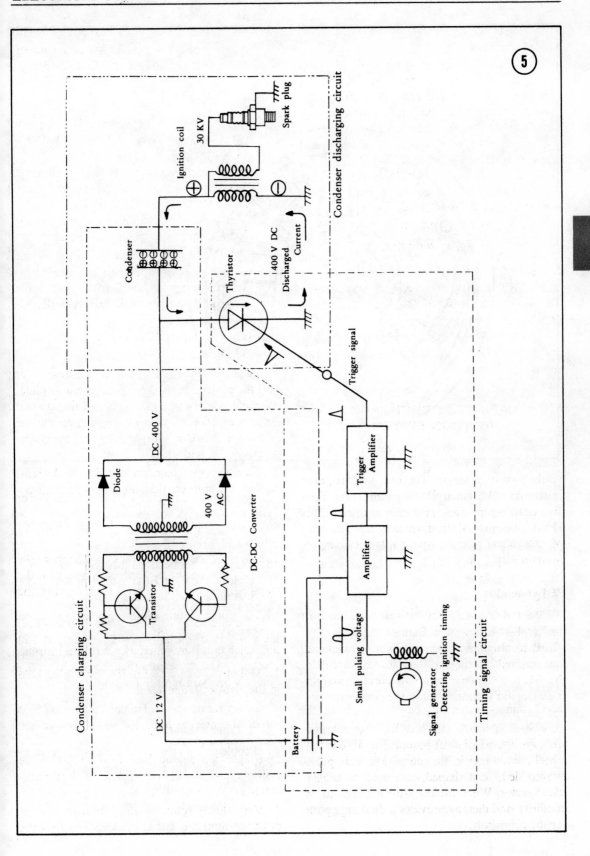

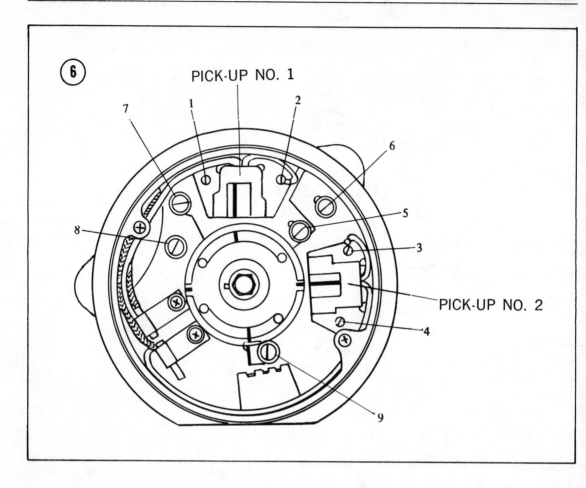

⑥

PICK-UP NO. 1

PICK-UP NO. 2

piston is 0.127 inch (3.28 millimeters) below top dead center. The crankshaft position will be 25 degrees before top dead center.

5. Be sure that the stamped line on the No. 2 pickup coil is roughly aligned with the stamped line on the rotor projection.

6. Bend the pointer with pliers so that the line at the bottom of the rotor aligns exactly with the pointer.

7. Perform steps (3) through (7) of the timing procedure.

CDI Cautions

Certain measures must be taken to protect the capacitor discharge system. Instantaneous damage to the semiconductors in the system will occur if the following precautions are not observed:

1. Never connect the battery backward. If the polarity is wrong, damage will occur to the rectifier and the alternator.

2. Do not disconnect the battery when the engine is running. A voltage surge will occur which will damage the rectifier and possibly burn out the lights.

3. Keep the connections between the various units clean and tight. Be sure that the wiring connectors are pushed together firmly.

4. Do not substitute another type of ignition coil or battery.

5. Each unit is mounted with a rubber vibration isolator. Always be sure that the isolators are in place when you replace the units.

CDI Troubleshooting

Problems with the capacitor discharge system fall into one of the following categories:

    a. Weak spark

    b. No spark

    c. Sparks occur at random

Symptom	Probable Cause	Remedy
Weak spark	Low battery	Charge battery
	Poor connections	Clean and tighten connections
	High voltage leakage	Replace defective wire
	Defective coil	Replace coil
	Unit "B" defective	Replace
No spark	Discharged battery	Charge battery
	Fuse burned out	Replace fuse
	Wiring broken	Repair wire
	Defective coil	Replace coil
	Unit "A" or "B" defective	Replace defective unit
	Defective signal generator coil	Replace signal generator coil
Random sparks	Unit "A" or "B" defective	Replace defective unit

Unit Tests

Although the most conclusive test can be made by substituting a known good unit for a suspected one, some tests may be made with a voltmeter, ammeter, and ohmmeter.

1. See **Figure 7** (p. 50). Measure the resistance between the black wire and the green or gray wire on unit "A". The ohmmeter must indicate infinity.

2. Reverse the meter connections. The meter must again indicate infinite resistance.

CAUTION
Unit "B" develops high voltage. Follow the procedure exactly to avoid shock hazard.

3. Connect unit "B" as shown in **Figure 8** (p. 50). Connect the brown wire to the negative terminal of the ammeter. Connect the positive terminal of the 12-volt battery to the positive terminal of the ammeter. Connect the black wire to the negative battery terminal.

4. The ammeter must indicate 1.8 plus or minus 0.5 amperes, and not fluctuate.

5. Disconnect the brown wire from the battery. Connect the negative lead on the voltmeter to the negative battery terminal. Connect the positive voltmeter lead to the green or gray wire.

6. Reconnect the brown wire to the battery. The voltmeter must indicate 370 to 500 volts.

7. It is normal that the unit emits a tone.

8. Disconnect the battery, then the voltmeter.

9. Connect both units together, as shown in **Figure 9** (page 51), but do not connect the battery.

10. Connect the voltmeter to the green or gray wire. It may be necessary to fabricate some suitable wires to connect the plugs and the voltmeter.

11. Connect the battery as in step (3).

12. If unit "B" checked okay earlier, but the ammeter does not indicate 1.8 plus or minus 0.5 amperes, or the voltmeter does not indicate 370 to 500 volts, unit "A" is defective.

ALTERNATOR

An alternator is a form of electrical generator in which a magnetized field called a rotor revolves within a set of stationary coils called a stator. As the rotor revolves, alternating current is induced in the stator. The current is then rectified and used to operate the electrical accessories on the motorcycle and for charging the battery. The rotor may be either permanently magnetized, or magnetized by a separate winding in the rotor. Kawasaki machines use both types. Alternators with permanently magnetized rotors are controlled by a solid state regulator. Alternators with externally excited field windings require a regulator similar to that in an automobile. **Figures 10 and 11** illustrate the two types of rotors used in Kawasaki machines. The rotor in Figure 10 is permanently magnetized; the rotor in Figure 11 requires separate excitation.

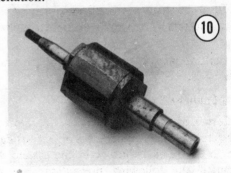

If alternator problems are suspected, as in the case of a chronically undercharged battery or dim headlights, check the alternator output voltage.

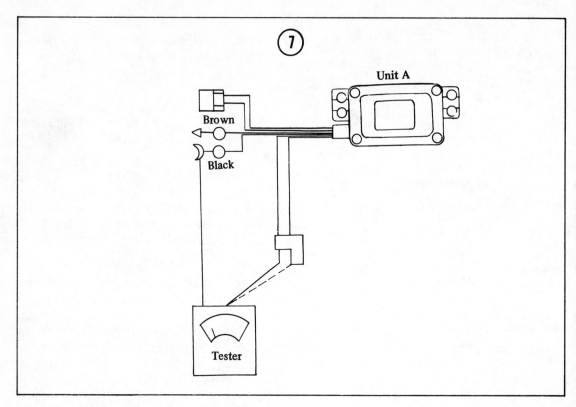

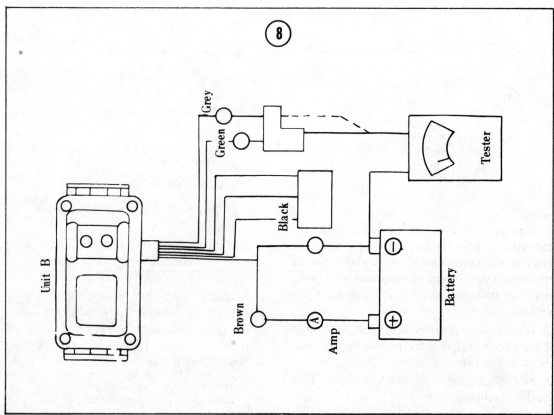

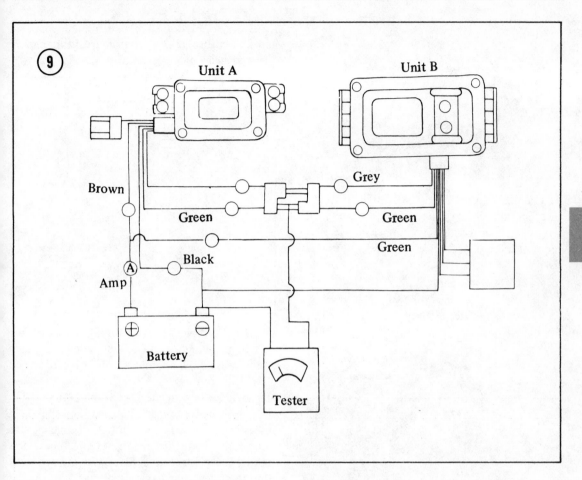

1. Connect a 0-20 DC voltmeter across the battery terminals. Be sure that you connect the positive voltmeter lead to the positive battery terminal, and the negative voltmeter lead to the negative battery terminal. Do not start the engine.

2. Observe the voltmeter indication and record it for reference during the next step. The voltmeter will indicate battery voltage.

3. Start engine and run it at 5,000 rpm. Turn on the headlights.

4. Again observe the voltmeter. If the meter indication is now approximately 1 to 1½ volts higher than the meter indication obtained in step (2), the alternator is good, and no further checks are required.

5. If the indication obtained in step (4) was less than one volt greater than the battery voltage obtained in step (2), further checking will be required.

If further testing is required, perform the following steps:

1. Measure field winding resistance between the slip rings, as shown in **Figure 12**. If the resistance is not 3.5 to 5.5 ohms, replace the rotor.

2. Measure insulation resistance of the field winding. Set the ohmmeter to its highest range, then measure resistance between either slip ring and the rotor shaft. Insulation resistance must be essentially infinite.

NOTE: *Steps 1 and 2 do not apply to alternators with permanently magnetized rotors.*

3. On machines with conventional breaker contact ignition system, check for continuity between each pair of leads coming from the alternator (**Figure 13**). Measure between the leads listed:

> Yellow - Green
> Yellow - Green/yellow
> Green - Green/yellow

If all indicate continuity, measure the insulation resistance between the yellow wire and the alternator housing (**Figure 14**). If the meter indicates infinite resistance, the stator coils are in good condition.

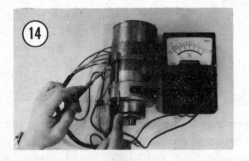

Adjusting a New Alternator

Whenever an alternator has been removed or installed on battery ignition models, it is necessary to make initial timing adjustments.

1. Refer to **Figure 15**. Align all the punched marks on the crankshaft primary gear, clutch primary gear, and alternator gear.

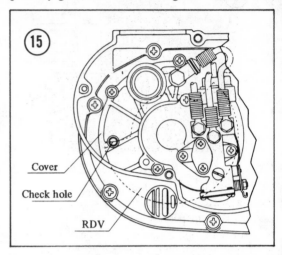

Cover
Check hole
RDV

There are two types of timing marks on the clutch gear (**Figure 16**). Engines with idler gears must use EN09 alternators for A1 series, and EN11 alternators for A7 series. In this case, use the two teeth with the dotted marks to set the idler gear between the clutch gear and the alternator gear. On engines without idler gears, use alternator model EN04 for A1 machines, and model EN08 for A7 machines. Use the two teeth on the clutch gear having "x" marks to set the alternator gear and the clutch gear.

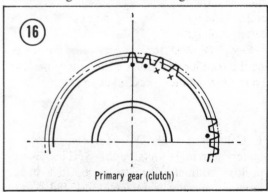

Primary gear (clutch)

Alignment of the clutch gear and primary gear is always the same, regardless of whether or not an idler gear is used.

2. Position the alternator on the crankcase so that the dowel pin holes align with the dowels in the crankcase.

3. Adjust the left-hand point gap and ignition timing as specified elsewhere in this chapter.

4. Remove the bolt from the inspection hole (**Figure 17**).

5. Rotate the engine counterclockwise so that the cutaway in the left rotary valve is in the center of the inspection hole.

6. Adjust the ignition timing pointer so that it is aligned with the red mark on the timing plate.

7. Further adjustments are made as described in the section on ignition timing.

RECTIFIER

The rectifier assembly serves two purposes. It converts alternating current produced by the alternator into direct current which is used to charge the battery. It also prevents discharge of the battery through the alternator when the engine isn't running, or at other times when the output voltage of the alternator is less than battery voltage.

Figure 18 illustrates the procedure for checking the rectifier on models with battery ignition. To test the rectifier, proceed as follows:

1. With an ohmmeter, check for continuity between each yellow wire and the two red wires. Record the meter indications.

2. Reverse the ohmmeter leads and repeat the measurements of step (1).

3. If each pair of measurements was essentially infinite in one direction and low in the reverse direction, proceed with steps (4) and (5). If any pair of measurements showed either high or low resistance in both directions, replace the rectifier assembly.

4. Measure the resistance between each yellow lead and the two black leads. Record the meter indications.

5. Reverse the meter leads and repeat the measurements.

6. If any pair of measurements obtained in steps (4) or (5) was either both high or both low, replace the rectifier assembly.

SOLID STATE VOLTAGE REGULATOR

Some machines are equipped with a solid state voltage regulator (SVR). This unit consists of a zener diode (ZD), a silicon controlled rectifier (SCR), and two resistors, as shown in **Figures 19 and 20**. Refer to these illustrations during the following discussion.

Operation

Assume that the main switch is closed. As engine·speed increases, output voltage from the alternator tends to increase. If the battery is fully charged, the voltage at the junction of R1 and R2 will tend to rise. If it reaches the zener voltage, approximately 15 volts, the zener diode conducts in the reverse direction, thereby triggering the silicon controlled rectifier (SCR). When the silicon controlled rectifier conducts, the alternator output is grounded, thereby reducing the output voltage to near zero. As the voltage at the junction of R1 and R2 drops, the zener diode ceases to conduct, and removes the trigger signal to the silicon controlled rectifier.

Checking the SVR

Refer to **Figure 21**. Connect a test lamp in series with a 12-volt battery, or use an ohmmeter to determine whether there is continuity between the yellow/green and black wires (**Figure 22**). The continuity test lamp should not light, or the ohmmeter should show no continuity. Reverse

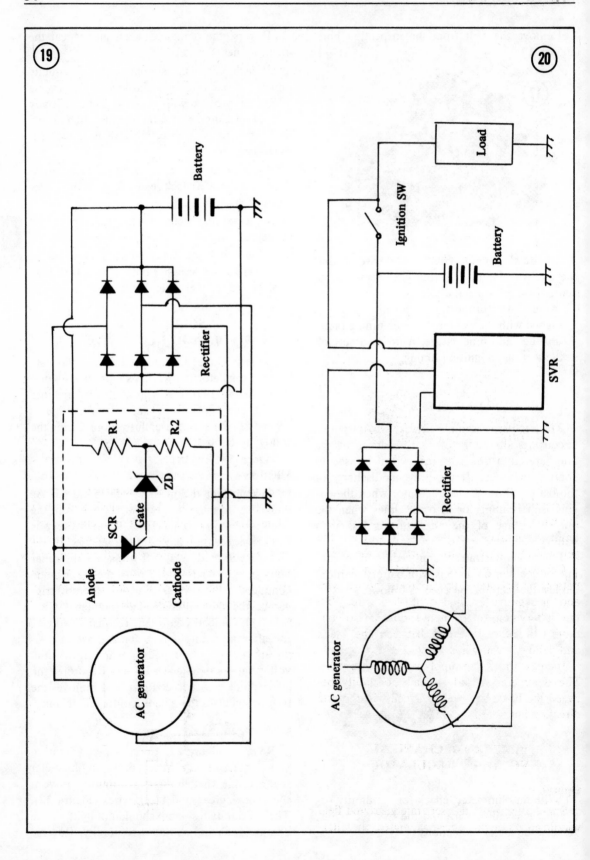

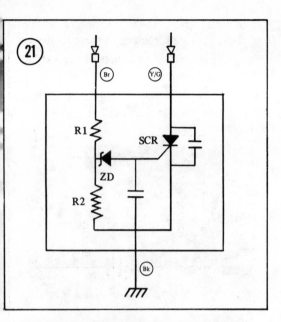

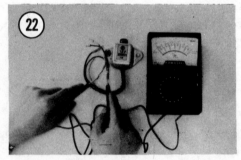

the continuity tester connections to the SVR. If the lamp lights or the ohmmeter indicates continuity, the unit is defective. Also be sure that the yellow/green wire is not shorted to the case.

Connect the positive terminal of a 12-volt battery or adjustable power to the brown wire and the negative terminal to the black wire. With the battery connected, there should be no continuity in either direction between the black and yellow/green wires.

Increase the power supply voltage to 16 volts. The ohmmeter should indicate continuity between the black and yellow/green wires in one direction but not in the other.

ELECTROMECHANICAL VOLTAGE REGULATOR

Operation

Some alternators use separately excited field windings. As engine speed increases, the alter-

nator output tends to increase. It is possible, however, to control the alternator output by controlling the field current.

Figure 23 illustrates the situation at low engine speeds. The rectified alternator output is applied to coil "B". However, since the output is low, the magnetic field developed by coil "E" is too low to open the black and white relay contacts. Under these conditions, field current is supplied by the battery through the ignition switch, and is at its maximum value.

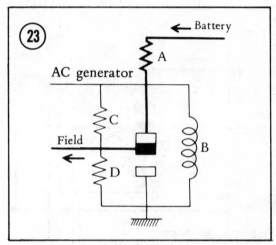

Figure 24 illustrates the circuit as engine speed increases. As the alternator output voltage tends to increase, coil "B" generates more magnetic force, which breaks the black and upper white contact. Field current is then supplied from the alternator output, through resistor "C". Resistor "C" limits the field current, and thereby reduces the alternator output so that the upper white contact and the black contact again close, repeating the cycle.

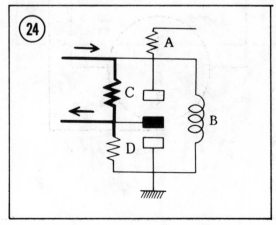

At high engine speeds and light electrical loads, the action of the upper and center contacts is insufficient to control the alternator output. **Figure 25** illustrates the regulator action under these conditions. As the output voltage continues to rise, coil "B" pulls the movable (black) contact down to the lower contact. Under this condition the field is grounded, and the alternator output drops to zero. As it drops, the movable and lower contacts separate, and the cycle repeats.

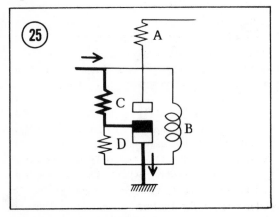

Testing the Regulator

The most common causes of voltage regulator trouble are open wires or short circuits. To check the regulator, proceed as follows:

1. Remove the four wires from the regulator.

2. With an ohmmeter (**Figure 26**) measure the resistance between the listed terminals. Resistance should be approximately as specified.

Terminals	Resistance
1 and 2	30 ohms
1 and 3	30 ohms
1 and 4	54 ohms

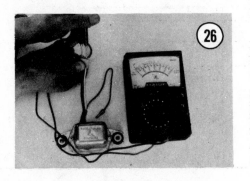

If the measured values are greatly different from those specified, replace the regulator.

3. Remove the cover and inspect the contacts for pitting or burning.

4. Connect a voltmeter across the battery terminals, as shown in **Figure 27**. Reconnect the regulator.

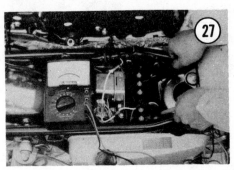

5. Start the engine and run it at 5,000 rpm. If the measured voltage is 14.5 plus or minus 0.5, the regulator is okay.

BATTERY

Maintenance

Check the battery occasionally for sulfation or deposits in the bottom of the cells. Replace the battery if such conditions exist, or if the battery will not accept or hold a charge.

Maintain the battery electrolyte level between the minimum and maximum level marks on the battery case. Use only distilled water to fill the cells. If the battery requires water more frequently than once a month, check the charging system, for it is possible that the battery is being overcharged.

Battery life should normally be two to three years. This period will be shortened by any of the following conditions:

1. Overcharging.

2. Leaving the battery in a discharged state.

3. Freezing—a fully charged battery will freeze at a much lower temperature than one that is discharged. If the machine is exposed to cold weather, be sure to keep the battery fully charged.

4. Allowing the electrolyte level to drop below the tops of the plates.

5. Adding anything to the electrolyte except distilled water.

If the motorcycle is not to be used for an extended period, charge the battery fully, remove it from the machine, and store it in a cool, dry place. Recharge the battery every two months while it is in storage, and again before it is put back into service.

Be very careful when you install the battery to connect it properly. If the battery is installed backward, the rectifier and alternator will be damaged. It is also possible that the CDI will be damaged.

Charging

Determine the state of charge of the battery with a hydrometer. To use this instrument, place the suction tube into the filter opening and draw in just enough electrolyte to lift the float. Hold the instrument in a vertical position and take the reading at eye level.

The specific gravity of the electrolyte varies with temperature, so it is necessary to apply a temperature correction to the reading you obtain. For each 10 degrees that the battery temperature exceeds 80 degrees F, add 0.004 to the indicated specific gravity. Subtract 0.004 from the indicated value for each 10 degrees that the battery temperature is below 80 degrees F.

The specific gravity of a fully charged battery is 1.260. If the specific gravity is below 1.220, recharge the battery.

LIGHTS

Machines which are intended to be ridden on public streets are equipped with lights. See **Figure 28** (next page). Check them periodically to be sure that they are working properly.

Headlight

The headlight unit consists primarily of a lamp body, a dual-filament bulb, a lens and a reflector unit, a rim, and a socket. To adjust the headlight, loosen the two mounting bulbs and move the assembly as required.

Brake Light

The switch is actuated by the brake pedal. Adjust the switch so that the stop light goes on just before braking action occurs. Move the switch body up or down as required for adjustment. Tighten the clamp nut after adjustment.

Turn Signals

Kawasaki machines are equipped with two different types of turn signal flasher relays. If replacement becomes necessary, be sure you replace with the proper type.

If any turn signal bulb burns out, be sure to replace it with the same type. Improper action of the flasher relay, or even failure to operate, may result from use of the wrong bulbs.

HORN

Current for the horn is supplied by the battery. One horn terminal is connected to the battery through the main switch. The other terminal is connected to the horn button. When the rider presses the button, current flows through the horn.

MAIN SWITCH

Service on the main switch is limited to checking for continuity between the various circuits. The following tables list the circuits which should show continuity under different switch positions.

Models With CDI	
Position	Leads connected
Off	None
Day	White and brown
Night	Red/white, white, brown, and blue
Parking	Red/white and white

Models With Battery Ignition	
Position	Leads connected
Off	None
Day	White and brown
Night	Red, white, brown, and blue
Twilight	Red, white, brown, and brown/white
Parking	Red, white, and brown/white

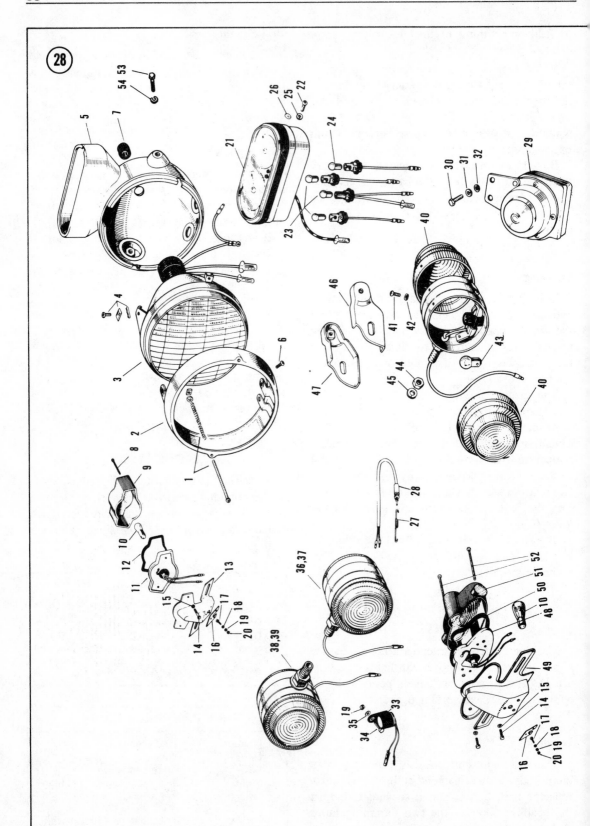

1. Focus adjusting screw
2. Headlight rim
3. Sealed beam unit
4. Sealed beam fitting screw
5. Headlight body
6. Oval countersunk screw
7. Wiring harness grommet
8. Pan head screw
9. Taillight lens
10. Taillight bulb
11. Taillight socket
12. Taillight gasket
13. License plate bracket
14. Hex bolt

15. Lockwasher
16. Taillight shock damper
17. Hex bolt
18. Lockwasher
19. Nut
20. Nut
21. Speedometer/tachometer
22. Pan head screw
23. Bulb
24. Bulb
25. Lockwasher
26. Flat washer
27. Brake light switch spring
28. Brake light switch

29. Horn
30. Hex bolt
31. Lockwasher
32. Nut
33. Turn signal relay
34. Hex bolt
35. Flat washer
36. Right turn signal lamp
37. Left turn signal lamp
38. Right rear turn signal lamp
39. Left rear turn signal lamp
40. Turn signal lamp lens
41. Pan head screw

42. Lockwasher
43. Bulb
44. Nut
45. Lockwasher
46. Left rear turn signal bracket
47. Right rear turn signal bracket
48. Taillight socket
49. License plate bracket
50. Taillight gasket
51. Taillight lens
52. Pan head screw
53. Headlight fitting bolt
54. Lockwasher

3

CHAPTER FOUR

CARBURETORS

For proper operation, a gasoline engine must be supplied with fuel and air, mixed in the proper proportions by weight. A mixture in which there is an excess of fuel is said to be rich. A lean mixture is one which contains insufficient fuel. It is the function of the carburetors to supply the proper mixture to the engine under all operating conditions.

Kawasaki twin-cylinder machines are equipped with one carburetor for each cylinder.

CARBURETOR OPERATION

Figure 1 (page 62) is an exploded view of a typical carburetor. The essential functional parts are a float and float valve mechanism for maintaining a constant fuel level in the float bowl, a pilot system for supplying fuel at low speeds, a main fuel system which supplies the engine at medium and high speeds, and a starter system, which supplies the very rich mixture needed to start a cold engine. The operation of each system is discussed in the following paragraphs.

Float Mechanism

Figures 2 and 3 illustrate a typical float mechanism. Proper operation of the carburetor is dependent on maintaining a constant fuel level in the carburetor bowl. As fuel is drawn from the float bowl, the float level drops. When the float

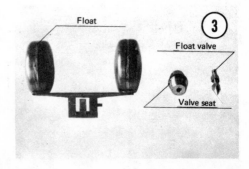

drops, the float valve moves away from its seat and allows fuel to flow past the valve into the float bowl. As this occurs, rises, eventually press the valve against its seat and shut off the flow of fuel. It can be seen from this discussion that a small piece of dirt can be trapped between the valve and seat, preventing the valve from closing and allowing fuel to rise beyond the normal level, resulting in flooding.

Pilot System

Under idle or low speed conditions, at less than one-eighth throttle, the engine doesn't require much fuel or air, and the throttle valve is almost closed. A separate pilot system is required for operation under such conditions. **Figure 4** illustrates the operation of the pilot system. Air is drawn through the pilot air inlet and controlled by the pilot air screw. The air is then

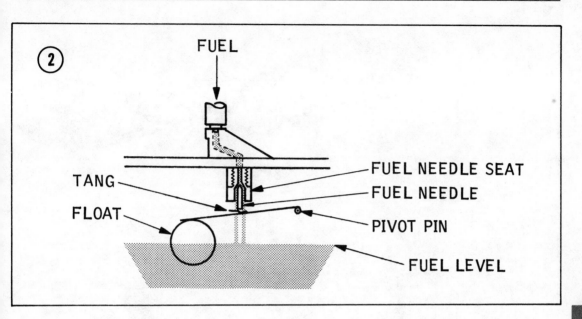

(2)

FUEL

TANG

FLOAT

FUEL NEEDLE SEAT
FUEL NEEDLE
PIVOT PIN
FUEL LEVEL

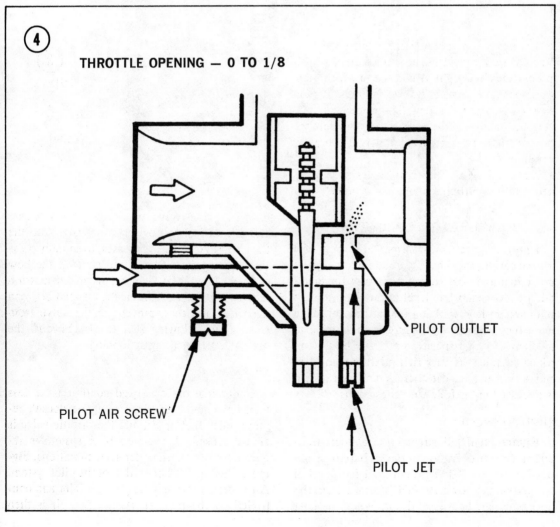

(4)

THROTTLE OPENING — 0 TO 1/8

PILOT OUTLET

PILOT AIR SCREW

PILOT JET

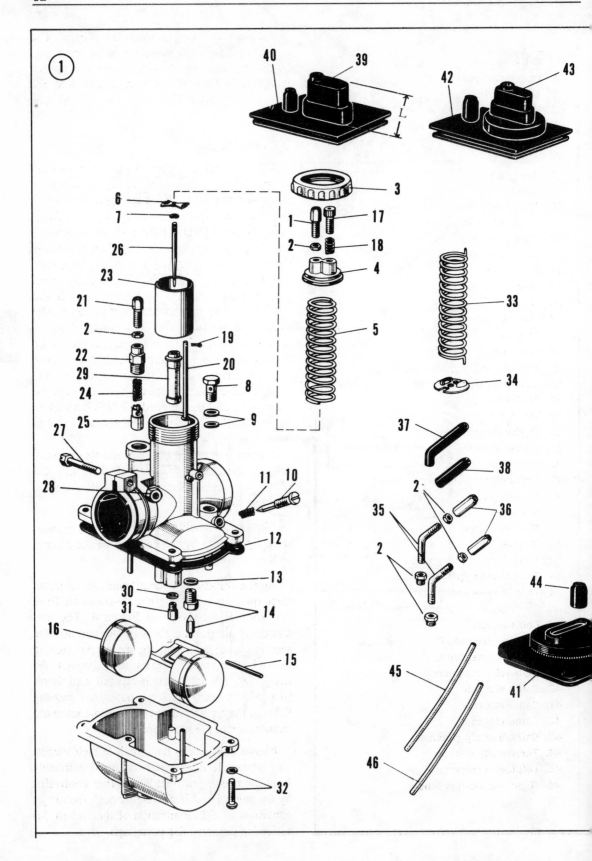

1. Cable adjuster
2. Cable adjuster lock nut
3. Mixing chamber cap
4. Mixing chamber top
5. Throttle valve spring
6. Throttle valve spring seat
7. Needle clip
8. Banjo bolt
9. Gasket
10. Pilot air adjusting screw
11. Adjusting screw spring
12. Float chamber gasket
13. Float valve seat washer
14. Float valve
15. Float pin
16. Float
17. Throttle adjuster
18. Throttle adjuster spring
19. Cotter pin
20. Throttle valve stop rod
21. Cable adjuster
22. Starter plunger cap
23. Throttle valve
24. Starter plunger spring
25. Starter plunger
26. Jet needle
27. Carburetor mounting clamp screw
28. Hex nut
29. Needle jet
30. Main jet washer
31. Main jet
32. Float chamber fitting screw
33. Throttle valve spring
34. Throttle valve spring seat
35. Cable guide
36. Cable adjuster
37. Cable adjuster cap B
38. Cable adjuster cap A
39. Carburetor cap grommet
40. Carburetor cap
41. Carburetor cap
42. Carburetor cap
43. Carburetor cap grommet
44. Throttle adjuster cap
45. Left fuel overflow tube
46. Right fuel overflow tube

mixed with fuel drawn through the pilot jet. The air/fuel mixture then travels from the pilot outlet into the main air passage, where it is further mixed with air prior to being drawn into the engine. The pilot air screw controls the idle mixture.

Main Fuel System

As the throttle is opened further, to about one-quarter open, the pilot circuit begins to supply less of the mixture to the engine, as the main fuel system, illustrated in **Figure 5**, begins to function. The main jet, the needle jet, the jet needle, and the air jet make up the main fuel circuit. As the throttle valve opens more than about one-eighth of its travel, air is drawn through the main port, and passes under the throttle valve in the main bore. The velocity of the air stream results in reduced pressure around the jet needle. Fuel then passes through the main jet, past the needle jet and jet needle, and into the air stream where it is atomized and sent to the engine. As the throttle valve opens, more air flows through the carburetor, and the jet needle, which is attached to the throttle slide, rises to permit more fuel to flow.

A portion of the air bled past the air jet passes through the needle jet bleed air inlet into the needle jet, where the air is mixed with the main air stram and atomized.

Airflow at small throttle openings is controlled primarily by the cutaway on the throttle slide.

As the throttle is opened wide, up to about three-quarters open, the circuit draws air from two sources, as shown in **Figure 6**. The first source is air passing through the venturi; the second source is through the air jet. Air passing through the venturi draws fuel through the needle jet. The jet needle is tapered, and therefore allows more fuel to pass. Air passing through the air jet passes to the needle jet to aid atomization of the fuel there.

Figure 7 illustrates the circuit at high speeds. The jet needle is withdrawn almost completely from the needle jet. Fuel flow is then controlled by the main jet. Air passing through the air jet continues to aid atomization of the fuel as described in the foregoing paragraph.

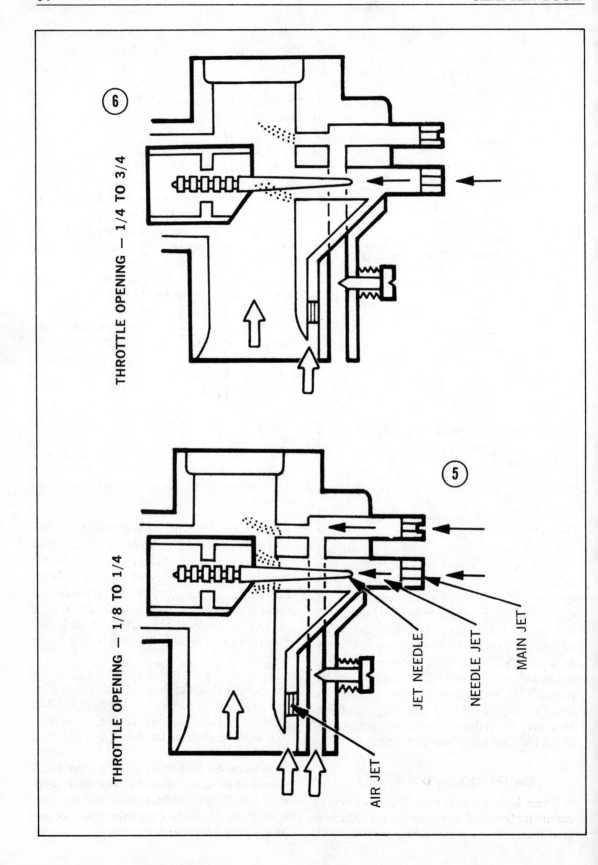

THROTTLE OPENING — 1/4 TO 3/4

⑥

THROTTLE OPENING — 1/8 TO 1/4

⑤

JET NEEDLE

NEEDLE JET

MAIN JET

AIR JET

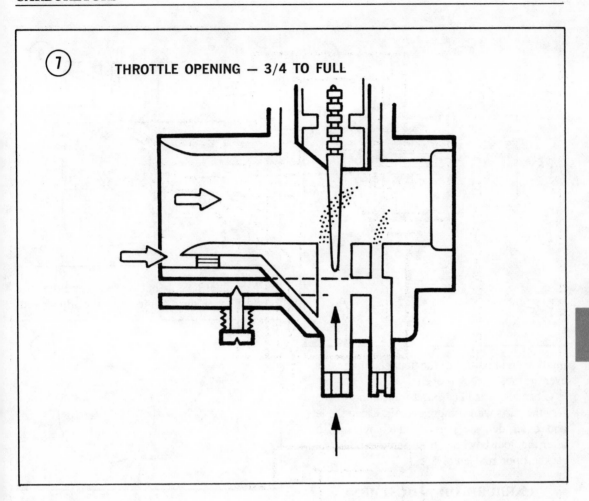

⑦ THROTTLE OPENING — 3/4 TO FULL

Starter System

A cold engine requires a far richer mixture than a warm one. **Figure 8** illustrates the starter system. When the rider operates the starter lever, the starter plunger (13) is pulled upward. As the engine is cranked, suction from the engine draws fuel through the starter jet (10). The fuel is then mixed with air from the bleed air port (11) in the float chamber (12). This mixture is further mixed with primary air which comes through the passage (14), and is then delivered to the engine through the port (15) behind the throttle valve. Note that the mixture from the starter system is mixed with that from the pilot system.

CARBURETOR OVERHAUL

There is no set rule regarding frequency of carburetor overhaul. A carburetor on a machine used primarily for street riding may go 5,000 miles without attention. Used in dirt, the carburetor might need an overhaul in less than 1,000 miles. Poor engine performance, hesitation, and little or no response to idle mixture adjustment are all symptoms of possible carburetor malfunction. As a general rule, its good practice to overhaul the carburetor each time you perform a routine decarbonization of the engine.

Remove the carburetor from the engine and disassemble it. Shake the float to check for gasoline inside. If fuel leaks into the float, the float chamber fuel level will rise, resulting in an over-rich mixture. Replace the float if it is deformed or leaking.

Replace the float valve if its seating end is scratched or worn. Press the float valve gently with your finger and make sure that the valve seats properly. If the float valve does not seat properly, fuel will overflow, causing an overrich

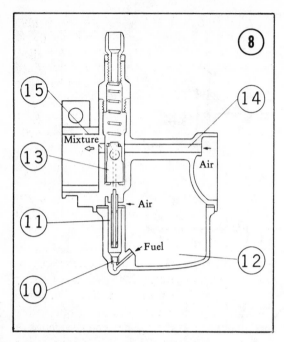

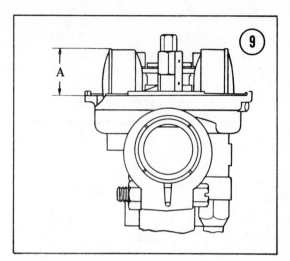

If the float level is not correct, bend the tang on the float (**Figure 10**) to make the adjustment.

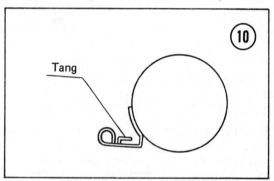

mixture and flooding of the float chamber whenever the fuel petcock is open.

Clean all parts in carburetor cleaning solvent. Dry the parts with compressed air. Clean the jets and other delicate parts with compressed air after the float bowl has been removed. Use new gaskets upon reassembly.

CARBURETOR ADJUSTMENT

Carburetor adjustment is not normally required except for occasional setting of idling speed, or at time of carburetor overhaul.

Float Level

The machine was delivered with the float level adjusted correctly. Rough riding, a bent float arm, or a worn float needle and seat can cause the float level to change.

Figure 9 illustrates the float level adjustment for these machines. Remove the carburetor, then remove the float chamber body. Measure distance "A" between the gasket surface and the top of the floats. Distance "A" must be equal for each float, and as listed in the following table.

Model	Distance "A"
A1 Series	1.06 - 1.14 in. (27-29mm)
A7 Series	1.14 - 1.22 in. (29-31mm)

Standard Settings

The following table lists standard carburetor specifications. These specifications have been developed after exhaustive tests, and should not be changed unless there is definite reason to do so.

Item	A1 Series	A7 Series
Type	VM22SC	VM28SC
Main jet	140	97.5
Needle jet	0-6	0-4
Jet needle	4J13-3	5E14-4
Pilot jet	30	30
Cutaway	2.5	1.5
Air screw	1½ turns open	1½ turns open

Idle Speed Adjustment

To adjust idle speed on the various models, refer to the foregoing table. First set the idle mixture screw by turning it in until it seats lightly. Next, back it out the number of turns specified. Finally, adjust the idle speed. At higher altitudes, above approximately 3,000 feet (1,000 meters), it may be advisable to back out the mixture screw an additional quarter turn.

A suggested method for adjusting the idle speed is to warm up the engine, then stop it and disconnect all but one spark plug lead. Restart the engine, then very slowly reduce the idle speed until the engine just dies. Repeat the procedure for each remaining cylinder. Reconnect the spark plug leads, and start the engine. Finally, adjust each idle speed screw equally to achieve the lowest stable idle speed.

Carburetor Synchronization

Power output from the cylinders will be unbalanced unless the carburetors are synchronized. If one cylinder receives more fuel/air mixture from its associated carburetor then the others, overall poor performance will result.

1. Remove the air filter connections.

2. Rotate the throttle grip to the full open position.

3. Look into the carburetor bores as you slowly rotate the throttle grip to the closed position. It may be helpful to use a small mirror to do so.

4. All slides must enter the carburetor bores at the same time. If they do not, use the cable adjuster at the top of the carburetor to raise or lower one slide to match the others.

Speed Range Adjustments

The carburetors on your machine were designed to provide the proper mixture under all operating conditions. Little or no benefit will result from experimenting. However, unusual operating conditions such as sustained operation at high altitudes or unusually high or low temperatures may make modifications to the standard specifications desirable. The adjustments described in the following paragraphs should only be undertaken if the rider has definite reason to believe they are required. Do not make any change to one carburetor without making a similar change to those remaining.

1. To adjust the carburetor for low speed operation, refer to Figure 4. With the engine warm and running at idle, open the throttle. If the engine does not accelerate smoothly from idle, turn each air screw in (clockwise) slightly to richen the mixture. If the condition still exists, return each air screw to its original position and replace each throttle valve with one having a smaller cutaway. If the engine operation is worsened by turning the air screws, replace each throttle valve with one having a larger cutaway.

2. For operation at throttle openings of one- to three-quarters, adjustment is made with the jet needles, as shown in Figure 6. To richen the mixture, place the jet needle clip in a lower groove. Conversely, placing the clip in a higher groove leans the mixture.

3. Figure 7 illustrates the fuel flow at and near full throttle operation. If at full throttle operation, the engine performs better when the starter lever is moved to the rich position, or when backing off, change the main jet to one with a larger number. If the engine shows evidence of running rich, change the main jet to one with a lower number.

Half throttle operation is controlled by the jet needle position, but main jet size has some influence also. For this reason, it is necessary to fifirst determine the main jet size. If half throttle tests show the mixture to be too lean, place the clip on the jet needle in a lower groove to richen the mixture. If the mixture at half throttle is too rich, place the clip in the next higher groove. Repeat the test as necessary.

Make road tests at full and at half throttle for the final determination of main jet size and jet needle position. Since main jet size affects half throttle operation, make the full throttle tests first. To make such tests, operate the machine under each such condition for at least two minutes, then shut the engine off, release the clutch, and allow the machine to stop. After each such test, remove and examine the spark plug. The insulator should be a light tan color.

Full throttle operation is controlled by the main jet. If spark plug examination shows that the mixture is too lean, try a main jet with a higher number. Conversely, if the mixture was too rich, use a smaller jet. As a general rule, the main jet size should be reduced approximately five percent for each 3,300 feet above sea level.

The following table lists symptoms caused by rich and lean mixtures:

4

Condition	Symptom
Rich Mixture	Rough idle
	Black exhaust smoke
	Hard starting, especially when hot
	"Blubbering" under acceleration
	Black deposits in exhaust pipe
	Gas-fouled spark plug
	Poor gas mileage
	Engine performs worse as it warms up
Lean Mixture	Backfiring
	Rough idle
	Overheating
	Hesitation upon acceleration
	Engine speed varies at fixed throttle
	Loss of power
	White color on spark plug insulator
	Poor acceleration
	Performance improves if starter lever is held open

A summary of carburetor adjustments is given in the following table:

Throttle Opening	Adjustment	If too Rich	If too Lean
0 - ⅛	Air screw	Turn out	Turn in
⅛ - ¼	Throttle valve cut-away	Use larger cutaway	Use smaller cutaway
¼ - ¾	Jet needle	Raise clip	Lower clip
¾ to full	Main jet	Use smaller number	Use larger number

CARBURETOR COMPONENTS

The following paragraphs describe the various carburetor components which may be changed to vary performance characteristics.

Throttle Valve

Figure 11 illustrates the throttle valve. The cutaway controls airflow at small throttle openings. Cutaway sizes are numbered. Larger numbers permit more air to flow at a given throttle opening and result in a leaner mixture. Conversely, smaller numbers result in richer mixture.

Jet Needle

The jet needle **(Figure 12)** together with the needle jet, controls the mixture at medium speeds. As the throttle valve rises to increase airflow through the carburetor, the jet needle rises with it. The tapered portion of the jet needle rises from the needle jet and allows more fuel to flow, providing the engine with the proper mixture at up to about three quarters throttle opening. The five grooves at the top of the jet needle permit adjustment of the mixture ratio in the medium speed range.

Needle Jet

The needle jet **(Figure 13)** operates with the jet needle. Several holes are drilled through the

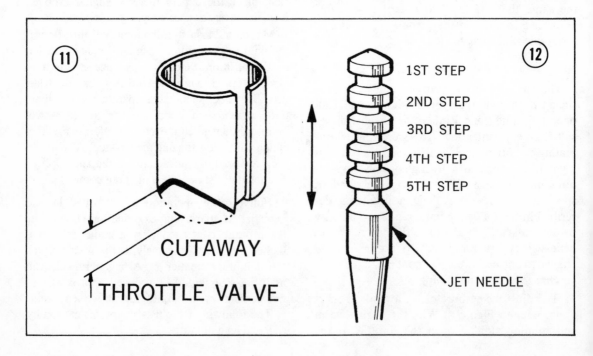

CUTAWAY

THROTTLE VALVE

1ST STEP
2ND STEP
3RD STEP
4TH STEP
5TH STEP

JET NEEDLE

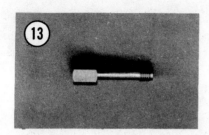

side of the needle jet. These holes meter the air-flow from the air jet. Air from the air jet is bled into needle jet to assist in atomization of fuel.

Main Jet

Figure 14 illustrates the main jet. The main jet controls the mixture at full throttle, and has some effect at lesser throttle openings. Each main jet is stamped with a number. Fuel flow is approximately proportional to the number. Larger numbers provide a richer mixture.

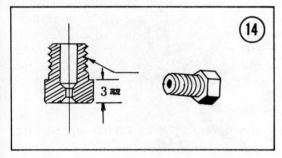

MISCELLANEOUS CARBURETOR PROBLEMS

Water in the carburetor float bowl and sticking carburetor slide valves can result from careless washing of the motorcycle. To remedy the problem, remove and clean the carburetor bowl, main jet, and any other affected parts. Be sure to cover the air intake when you wash the machine.

Be sure that the ring nut on top of each carburetor is neither too tight nor too lose. If the carburetor mounting cinch bolt is loose, the carburetor can pivot, resulting in an improper mixture because the float level is changed.

If gasoline leaks past the float bowl gasket, high speed fuel starvation may occur. Varnish deposits on the outside of the float bowl point to this condition.

Dirt in the fuel may lodge in the float valve and cause an overrich mixture. As a temporary measure, tap the carburetor lightly with any convenient tool to dislodge the dirt. Clean the fuel tank, petcock, fuel line, and carburetor at the first opportunity, should this occur.

Check the starter plunger occasionally. The neoprene seal on the bottom may become damaged. If this occurs, fuel will leak into the chamber and eventually work its way into the carburetor venturi, causing the machine to run rich.

4

CHAPTER FIVE

CHASSIS, SUSPENSION, AND STEERING

FRAME

Frames on these machines are of welded steel tubing. **Figure 1** (next page) illustrates the frame. The double loop construction of the frame results in light weight and rigidity.

Service on the frame is limited to inspection for bending or cracked welds. Examine the frame carefully in the event that the machine has been in a collision or had a hard spill.

HANDLEBAR

The handlebar is made from solid drawn steel tubing. Most of the manual controls (**Figure 2**, p. 72) are mounted on the handlebar assembly. Wiring from the switches on the handlebar assembly is routed to the headlight assembly, where it is connected to the main wiring harness.

Disassembly

1. Loosen the clutch cable lock nut (**Figure 3**), then rotate the adjustment nut to provide the inner clutch cable with sufficient slack to remove the clutch cable from the lever.

2. Loosen the front brake adjustment nut (see **Figure 4**), then remove the brake cable (**Figure 5**) from the brake lever on the handlebar.

3. Remove the throttle cables from the carburetors, as shown in **Figure 6**.

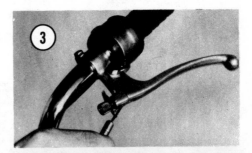

Adjusting nut

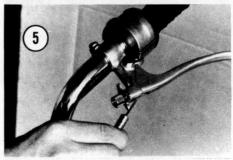

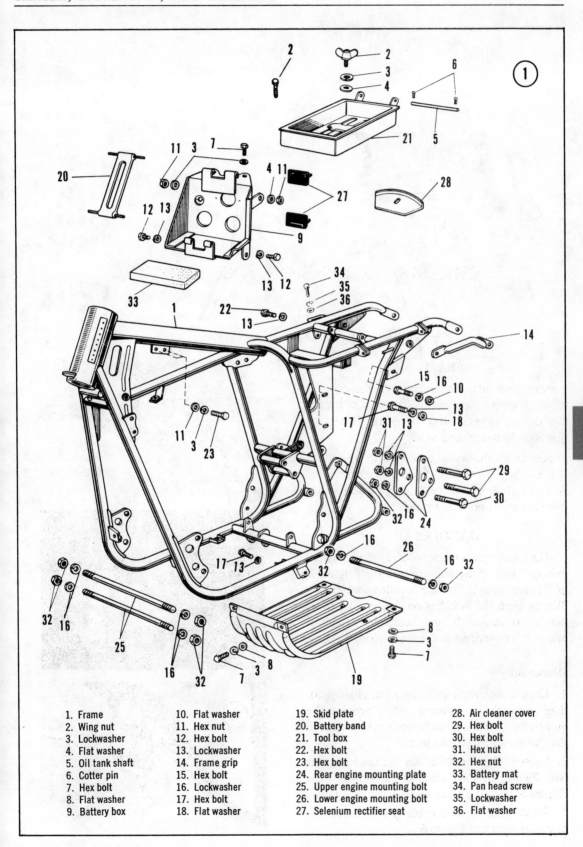

1. Frame
2. Wing nut
3. Lockwasher
4. Flat washer
5. Oil tank shaft
6. Cotter pin
7. Hex bolt
8. Flat washer
9. Battery box
10. Flat washer
11. Hex nut
12. Hex bolt
13. Lockwasher
14. Frame grip
15. Hex bolt
16. Lockwasher
17. Hex bolt
18. Flat washer
19. Skid plate
20. Battery band
21. Tool box
22. Hex bolt
23. Hex bolt
24. Rear engine mounting plate
25. Upper engine mounting bolt
26. Lower engine mounting bolt
27. Selenium rectifier seat
28. Air cleaner cover
29. Hex bolt
30. Hex bolt
31. Hex nut
32. Hex nut
33. Battery mat
34. Pan head screw
35. Lockwasher
36. Flat washer

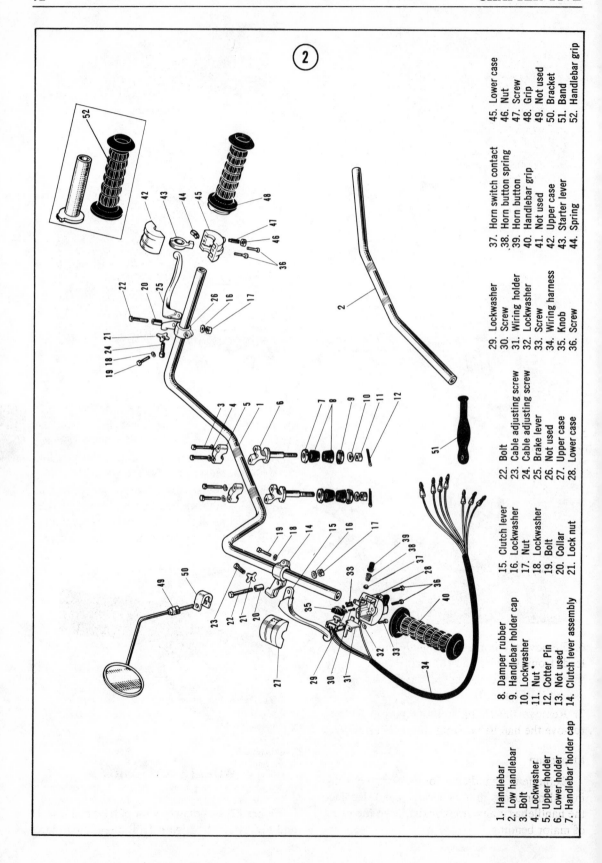

1. Handlebar
2. Low handlebar
3. Bolt
4. Lockwasher
5. Upper holder
6. Lower holder
7. Handlebar holder cap

8. Damper rubber
9. Handlebar holder cap
10. Lockwasher
11. Nut
12. Cotter Pin
13. Not used
14. Clutch lever assembly

15. Clutch lever
16. Lockwasher
17. Nut
18. Lockwasher
19. Bolt
20. Collar
21. Lock nut

22. Bolt
23. Cable adjusting screw
24. Cable adjusting screw
25. Brake lever
26. Not used
27. Upper case
28. Lower case

29. Lockwasher
30. Screw
31. Wiring holder
32. Lockwasher
33. Screw
34. Wiring harness
35. Knob
36. Screw

37. Horn switch contact
38. Horn button spring
39. Horn button
40. Handlebar grip
41. Not used
42. Upper case
43. Starter lever
44. Spring

45. Lower case
46. Nut
47. Screw
48. Grip
49. Not used
50. Bracket
51. Band
52. Handlebar grip

4. Disassemble the throttle grip assembly (**Figure 7**), then remove the control cable.

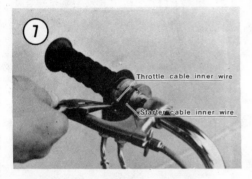

Throttle cable inner wire
Starter cable inner wire

5. Disassemble the starter lever (**Figure 8**), then remove the starter cable.

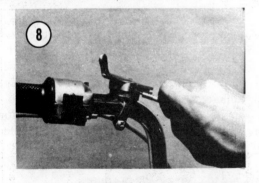

6. Remove the horn, turn signal, and headlight leads from the wire harness inside the headlight assembly, then disassemble the left-hand grip assembly (**Figure 9**).

7. Remove the clamp bolts (**Figure 10**), then remove the handlebar from the bracket.

Inspection

Examine the handlebar for cracking or bending. Minor bends may be straightened. Replace the handlebar if any cracks exist, or in the event of major bending.

Installation

Reverse the removal procedure to install the handlebar. Pass the wiring through the handlebar tubing and through the cord protector in the headlight. After installation, adjust the play in the throttle, clutch, and starter lever cables. Adjust the play in the front brake lever to 0.8 to 1.2 inches (20 to 30 millimeters) by means of the brake adjusting nut on the brake. Adjust the throttle grip with the adjustment screw (**Figure 11**), as desired.

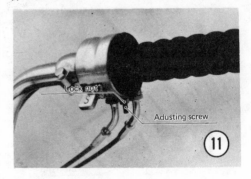

Lock nut
Adusting screw

WHEELS AND TIRES

Tires

Figure 12 is a cutaway view of a typical wheel and tire assembly. **Figure 13** is a sectional view

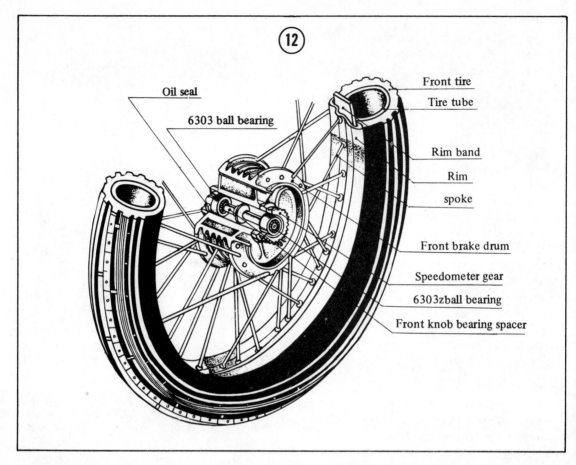

⑫

Oil seal

6303 ball bearing

Front tire

Tire tube

Rim band

Rim

spoke

Front brake drum

Speedometer gear

6303zball bearing

Front knob bearing spacer

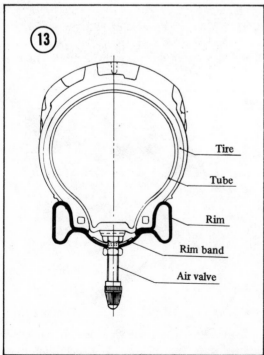

⑬

Tire

Tube

Rim

Rim band

Air valve

of a tire mounted on its rim. Various tire sizes are fitted to Kawasaki machines. Refer to the specifications for tire sizes for your machine. Tires are available in different tread types to suit the different requirements of the rider. The following table lists the normal tire pressures for the various models, measured with the tires cold. It is normal for tire pressure to increase after prolonged operation. Do not bleed air from a hot tire to decrease the pressure.

NOTE: *Adjust tire pressure on models A1R and A7R to suit the course.*

Check the tires periodically for wear, bruises, cuts, or other damage. Remove any small stones which may lodge in the tread, with a small screwdriver or similar tool.

Rims

The rim supports the tire and provides rigidity to the wheel assembly. A rim band protects the inner tube from abrasion.

Spokes

The spokes support the weight of the motorcycle and rider, and transmit tractive and braking forces, as shown in **Figure 14**. Diagram A illustrates action of the spokes as they support the machine. Tractive forces are shown in diagram B. Braking forces are shown in diagram C.

Check the spokes periodically for looseness or binding. A bent or otherwise faulty spoke will adversely affect neighboring spokes, and should therefore be replaced immediately. To remove the spoke, completely unscrew the threaded portion, then remove the bent end from the hub.

Spokes tend to loosen as the machine is used. Retighten each spoke one turn, beginning with those on one side of the hub, then those on the other side. Tighten the spokes on a new machine after the first 50 miles of operation, then at 50-mile intervals until they no longer loosen.

If the machine is subjected to particularly severe service, as in off-road or competition riding, check the spokes frequently.

Bead Protector

Some machines are equipped with a bead protector (**Figure 15A**) on each wheel. The bead protector prevents the tire from slipping on the rim, especially during maximum effort braking at high speeds, and thereby prevents damage to the valve stem.

Wheel Balance

An unbalanced wheel results in unsafe riding conditions. Depending on the degree of unbal-

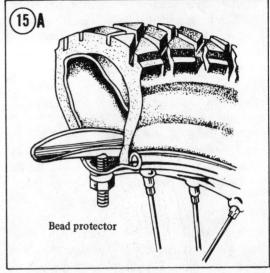

Bead protector

ance and the speed of the motorcycle, the rider may experience anything from a mild vibration to a violent shimmy which may even result in loss of control. Balance weights (**Figure 15B**) are applied to the spokes on the light side of the wheel to correct this condition.

Balance weights

5

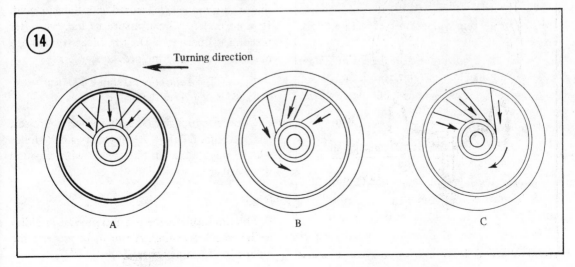

Turning direction

A   B   C

Before you attempt to balance the wheel, check to be sure that the wheel bearings are in good condition and properly lubricated, and that the brakes do not drag, so that the wheel rotates freely. With the wheel free of the ground, spin it slowly and allow it to come to rest by itself. Add balance weights to the spokes on the light side as required, so that the wheel comes to rest at a different position each time it is spun. Balance weights are available in weights of 10, 20, and 30 grams. Remove the drive chain when you balance the rear wheel.

Front Hub

Figure 16 is an exploded view of a typical front hub. The entire hub asembly rotates on two ball bearings. The speedometer gears transmit the front wheel rotation to the speedometer. The brake panel supports the brake mechanism.

Rear Hub

An exploded view of the rear hub is shown in **Figure 17** (p. 78). The rear hub consists of four major parts: the brake drum, the brake panel, the sprocket coupling, and the rear sprocket. The rear wheel bearings are mounted in the brake drum. The brake panel supports the brake mechanism, except for the brake drum. The sprocket coupling absorbs shocks throughout the entire drive train. The sprocket transmits engine power to the rear wheel through the sprocket coupling.

Front Wheel Removal

Front wheel removal is similar for all models. Proceed as follows:

1. Loosen the front brake adjustment nut, then remove the brake cable at the front hub.

2. Remove the speedometer cable bolt (shown in **Figure 18**), then pull out the speedometer cable (**Figure 19**).

3. Raise the front of the motorcycle and support it on a box or stand under the engine.

4. Remove the axle shaft pinch bolt (**Figure 20**).

5. Remove the front hub axle shaft nut (**Figure 21**) on the side of the front brake panel.

6. Pull out the axle shaft and remove the wheel from the motorcycle.

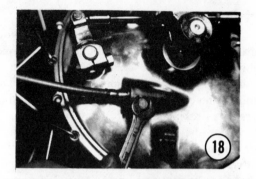

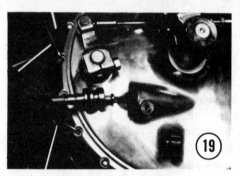

Rear Wheel Removal

1. Remove the rear brake adjustment nut (**Figure 22**), then remove the inner brake cable from the brake lever.

2. Remove the torque link (**Figure 23**).

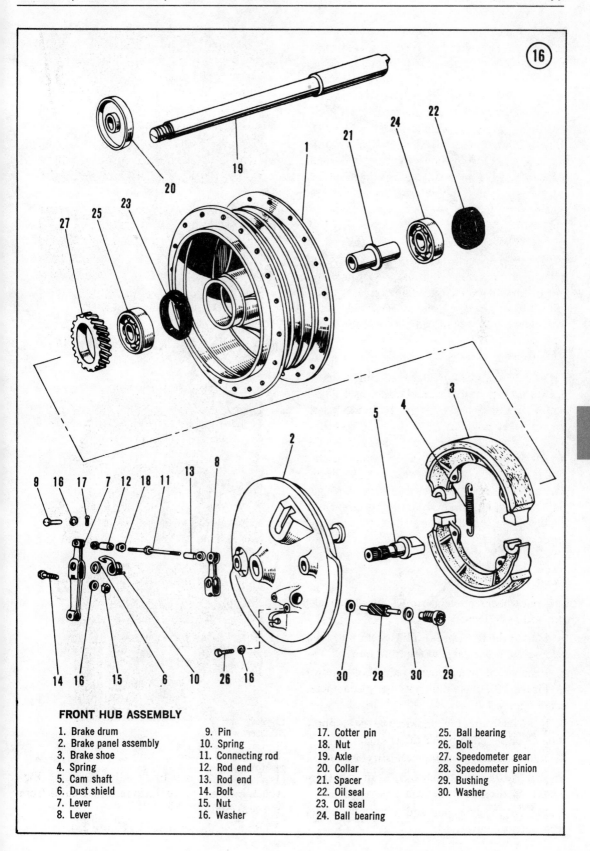

FRONT HUB ASSEMBLY

1. Brake drum
2. Brake panel assembly
3. Brake shoe
4. Spring
5. Cam shaft
6. Dust shield
7. Lever
8. Lever
9. Pin
10. Spring
11. Connecting rod
12. Rod end
13. Rod end
14. Bolt
15. Nut
16. Washer
17. Cotter pin
18. Nut
19. Axle
20. Collar
21. Spacer
22. Oil seal
23. Oil seal
24. Ball bearing
25. Ball bearing
26. Bolt
27. Speedometer gear
28. Speedometer pinion
29. Bushing
30. Washer

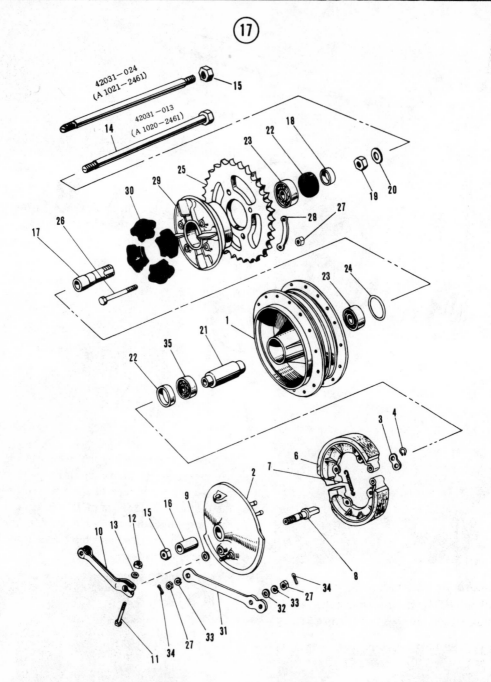

1. Rear brake drum
2. Rear brake panel
3. Rear brake shoe pin washer
4. Circlip
6. Rear brake shoe
7. Brake shoe spring
8. Rear brake cam
9. Brake cam dust shield
10. Rear brake cam lever
11. Hex bolt
12. Hex nut
13. Flat washer
14. Rear axle
15. Hex nut
16. Right rear hub collar
17. Rear axle sleeve
18. Rear axle sleeve collar
19. Sleeve nut
20. Sleeve washer
21. Rear hub bearing spacer
22. Oil seal
23. Ball bearing
24. O-ring
25. Rear sprocket
26. Rear sprocket fitting bolt
27. Hex nut
28. Sprocket lockwasher
29. Rear hub coupling
30. Rear hub shock damper
31. Rear brake torque link
32. Flat washer
33. Lockwasher
34. Cotter pin
35. Ball bearing

3. Loosen the chain tension adjustment bolts (**Figure 24**).

4. Remove the axle shaft nut (**Figure 25**).
5. Pull out the shaft, then remove the wheel and rear brake assembly together (**Figure 26**).

Wheel Disassembly

1. Lift the brake shoes, as shown in **Figure 27**, to remove them from the brake panel. The brake shoes and retracting springs will come out together.

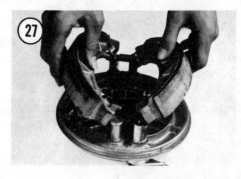

2. Insert a long drift punch (**Figure 28**) from the inner side of the brake drum, with its end against the inner race of the wheel bearing on the opposite side. Drive out the bearing and oil seal together. Be sure to reposition the drift punch after each hammer blow so that the bearing does not cock in its bore.

3. Insert the drift punch from the other side of the brake drum, then repeat step (2) to drive out the other bearing.

Inspection

1. Support each wheel shaft in a lathe, V-blocks, or other suitable centering device as shown in **Figure 29**. Rotate the shaft through a complete revolution. Straighten or replace the shaft if it is bent more than 0.02 inch (0.5 millimeter).

2. Check the inner and outer races of the wheel bearings for cracks, galling, or pitting. Rotate the bearings by hand and check for roughness. Replace the bearings if they are worn or damaged.

3. Inspect the main and auxiliary lips of the oil seal for wear or damage. Replace the oil seal if there is any doubt about its condition.

4. Inspect the rubber shock dampers in the rear hub. Replace the dampers if they are worn or damaged.

Wheel Reassembly

Reverse the disassembly procedure to reassemble the wheels. Observe the following notes as you reassemble the wheel.

1. Clean the wheel bearings carefully, then lubricate them before you install them.

2. Use an arbor press to install the bearings and oil seals. Be sure that the bearings and seals are seated squarely in their bores. Grease the oil seal lips upon assembly.

3. Be sure that there are no scratches, oil, or grease on the inner surface of the brake drum, or on the friction surfaces of the brake shoes. Clean the contact surfaces thoroughly with lacquer thinner before assembly.

4. The rubber shock dampers are tapered. Be sure that they are not reversed as you install them.

5. Tighten the axle shaft nuts as follows:

Model	Rear	Front
A Series	65-93 ft-lb (9-13 kg-m)	44-58 ft-lb (6-8 kg-m)

6. Check the wheels for runout after assembly.

Checking Wheel Runout

To measure runout of the wheel rim, support the wheel so that it is free to rotate. Position a dial indicator as shown in **Figure 30**. Observe the dial indicator as you rotate the wheel through a complete revolution. The runout limit for all models is 0.12 inch (3.0 millimeters). Excessive runout may be caused by a bent rim or loose spokes. Repair or replace them as required.

BRAKES

Each brake consists of a brake pedal or lever, cable, brake panel assembly, and brake drum. The brake panel assembly consists of the cam lever, cam shaft, brake shoes, retracting springs, and brake panel body. Front brakes are of the dual leading shoe type. The rear brakes have one leading and one trailing shoe. Both brakes are equipped with stop light switches (**Figures 31 and 32**).

Front Brake

The front brake mechanism is shown in **Figure 33**. Two cam shafts are used, one for each brake shoe. As each cam shaft turns, it forces its associated shoe into contact with the brake drum. Notice that as the brake drum turns counterclockwise, the movement of the brake drum tends to increase the pressure of the brake shoe against the drum, thereby increasing the braking power. Because of the self-energizing action of both brake shoes, this brake arrangement is somtimes called a dual leading shoe type.

Rear Brake

Figure 34 illustrates the rear brake. There is only one cam shaft which operates both brake shoes. When the cam shaft turns, it forces both shoes against the brake drum. The movement of the brake drum tends to increase the pressure of the forward shoe against the drum, therefore the forward shoe is a leading shoe because of the self-energizing effect. The rear shoe, however, makes contact with the drum opposite the direction of drum rotation, and the self-energizing effect does not occur. Therefore, the rear brake shoe is a trailing shoe.

Brake Inspection

Measure the inner diameter of the brake drum, as shown in **Figure 35**. Brake drum wear limits are listed in the following table. Replace the drum if it is worn beyond the service limit.

Model	Standard Value		Repair Limit	
	Front Inches (Millimeters)	Rear Inches (Millimeters)	Front Inches (Millimeters)	Rear Inches (Millimeters)
A Series	7.08 (180)	7.08 (180)	7.12 (180.75)	7.12 (180.75)

Examine the brake lining for oil or other foreign material. Replace any oll-soaked lining immediately. Dirt imbedded in the brake lining

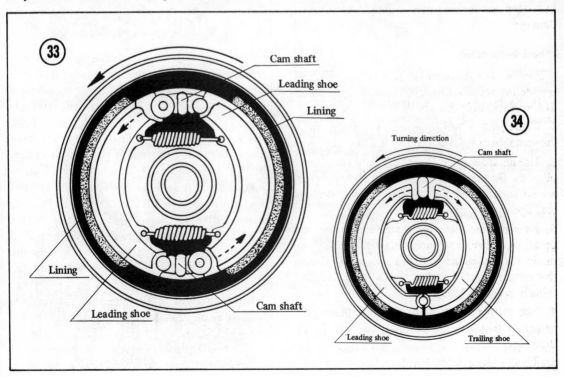

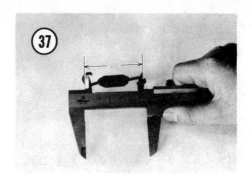

may be removed with a wire brush. Measure the thickness of the brake lining (**Figure 36**) at the thinnest part. Standard thickness for all models is 0.192 inch (5 millimeters). Replace both shoes if the thinnest portion of the lining on either shoe is worn to 0.118 inch (3 millimeters).

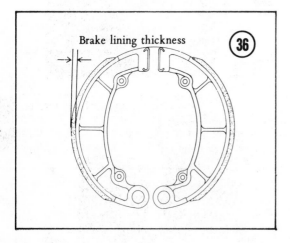

Brake lining thickness

If the brake shoe return spring is worn or stretched, the brake shoes will not retract fully and the brakes may drag. Measure the free length (**Figure 37**) of the return spring. Replace the spring if it is stretched beyond the repair limit.

Model	Standard Value		Repair Limit	
	Front	Rear	Front	Rear
	Inches	Inches	Inches	Inches
	(Millimeters)	(Millimeters)	(Millimeters)	(Millimeters)
A Series	1.80	2.2	1.92	2.32
	(46)	(56)	(49)	(59)

Measure the clearance between the brake cam shaft and the bushing in the brake panel. Standard clearance for all models is 0.0008 to

0.0028 inch (0.02 to 0.07 millimeter). Replace the cam shaft and/or the brake panel if clearance exceeds 0.02 inch (0.5 millimeter).

Brake Reassembly

To reassemble the brake mechanism, reverse the disassembly procedure. Be sure that the front brake cable is approximately perpendicular to the brake cam lever (**Figure 38**). Be sure to grease the brake pedal bearing, brake lever, and the brake cam shaft bearings in the brake panels.

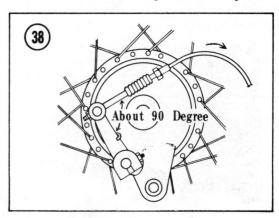

About 90 Degree

Brake Adjustment

Adjust the front brake by turning the adjustment nut at the front brake cam lever. The adjustment is correct when braking action begins when the front brake lever (**Figure 39**) is pulled approximately 1 inch (25 millimeters). Since the front brake stop lamp switch is built into the cable, no adjustment is required.

Adjust the rear brake by turning the adjustment nut until braking action begins at 1.0 to 1.4 inches (25 to 35 millimeters) travel of the brake pedal. Adjust the rear brake stop lamp switch (**Figure 40**) so that the stop lamp lights when

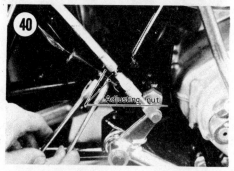

the brake pedal has traveled 0.6 to 0.8 inch (15 to 20 millimeters) as shown in **Figure 41**.

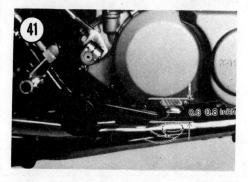

Adjustment of the front brake lever connecting rod is normally not required, except after replacement of the brake shoes. To adjust the lever, proceed as follows:

1. Support the machine so that the front wheel is clear of the ground.

2. Remove the brake lever connecting rod.

3. Spin the front wheel, then tighten the adjustment nut until the front brake drags very slightly.

4. Replace the connecting rod, then shorten or lengthen it as required so that the second brake shoe makes contact with the drum. Brake drag will increase at this point.

5. Readjust the front brake.

FRONT FORKS

An exploded view of the fork is shown in **Figure 42** (next page). The fork legs are oil damped, with internal springs.

Fork Removal

The initial steps for fork removal are similar for all models. Proceed as follows:

1. Remove all connectors in the headlight assembly from the main wire harness.

2. Remove the headlight assembly (**Figure 43**).

3. Remove the speedometer and tachometer, as shown in **Figure 44**.

4. Remove the cotter pin and nut at the lower end of the steering damper rod (**Figure 45**).

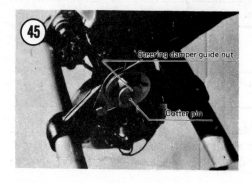

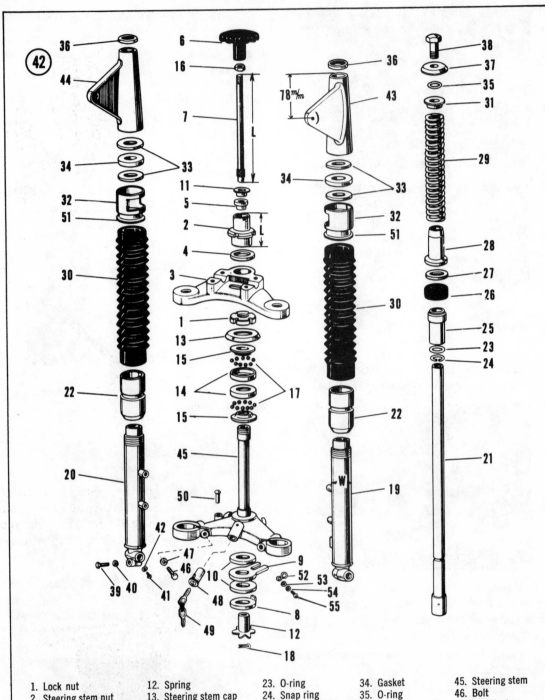

1. Lock nut
2. Steering stem nut
3. Steering steam head
4. Washer
5. Bushing
6. Damper knob
7. Rod
8. Disc
9. Stopper
10. Friction disc
11. Washer

12. Spring
13. Steering stem cap
14. Cup
15. Race
16. Lock nut
17. Ball
18. Cotter pin
19. Fork outer tube
20. Fork outer tube
21. Fork inner tube
22. Tube nut

23. O-ring
24. Snap ring
25. Guide
26. Oil seal
27. Washer
28. Dust shield
29. Spring
30. Dust cover
31. Spring guide
32. Cover guide
33. Washer

34. Gasket
35. O-ring
36. Cap
37. Washer
38. Bolt
39. Bolt
40. Lockwasher
41. Screw
42. Gasket
43. Fork cover
44. Fork cover

45. Steering stem
46. Bolt
47. Lockwasher
48. Lock assembly
49. Key set
50. Rivet
51. Dust cover holder
52. Clamp
53. Washer
54. Lockwasher
55. Screw

Then loosen the steering damper knob (see **Figure 46**) and remove the steering damper.

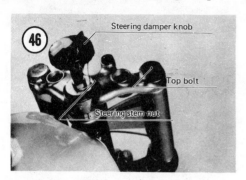

5. Remove the steering stem nut (**Figure 47**) with the special spanner wrench (**Figure 48**).

6. Remove the top bolts (**Figure 49**).

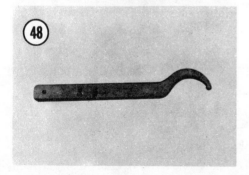

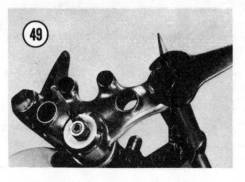

7. Remove the underbracket bolts (**Figure 50**), then pull out the fork legs .

Fork Disassembly

1. Insert the fork and drain the oil, as shown in **Figure 51**.

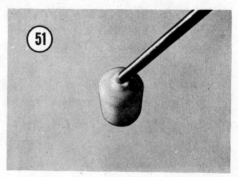

2. Wrap a piece of rubber sheeting or section of inner tube around the outer tube nut, then clamp the nut in a vise (**Figure 52**). Be careful that you do not deform the tube by clamping the vise too tightly.

3. Turn the outer tube counterclockwise to separate the tubes. The outer tube may be turned easily by using the front axle shaft as a lever, as shown in **Figure 53**.

5

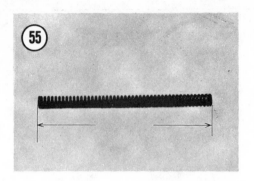

Inspection

1. Assemble the inner and outer tubes as shown in **Figure 54**, then slide them together. Check for looseness, noise, or binding. Replace any defective parts.

2. Any scratches or roughness on the inner tube in the area where it passes through the oil seal will damage the oil seal. Examine this area carefully.

3. Inspect the dust seal carefully. If this seal is damaged, foreign material will enter the fork.

4. Measure the free length of each fork spring (**Figure 55**). Replace any spring which is shorter than the repair limit.

Model	Standard Value		Service Limit	
	Inches	(Millimeters)	Inches	(Millimeters)
A Series	8.0	(202.5)	7.56	(192)

Fork Reassembly

Reverse the disassembly procedure to reassemble the fork. Be sure to replace the oil seal and O-ring which are attached to the outer tube nut.

Fork Installation

Insert the fork through the lower part of the steering stem, then pull it into position with the fork tool, then temporarily tighten the steering stem bolt (**Figure 56**). Install the top bolt, then again loosen the steering stem bolt and check the fork for play. Finally, retighten the top bolt, then the steering stem bolt.

Front Fork Oil

Change the front fork oil initially at 300 miles (500 kilometers) and at every 3,000 miles (5,000 kilometers) thereafter. Mix one part 60-weight spindle oil to four parts 30-weight engine oil. Then pour 0.2 quart (210 cubic centimeters) into each fork leg.

STEERING SYSTEM

Figure 57 is a sectional view of a typical steering stem. The frame head pipe and the underbracket are provided with ball bearings for

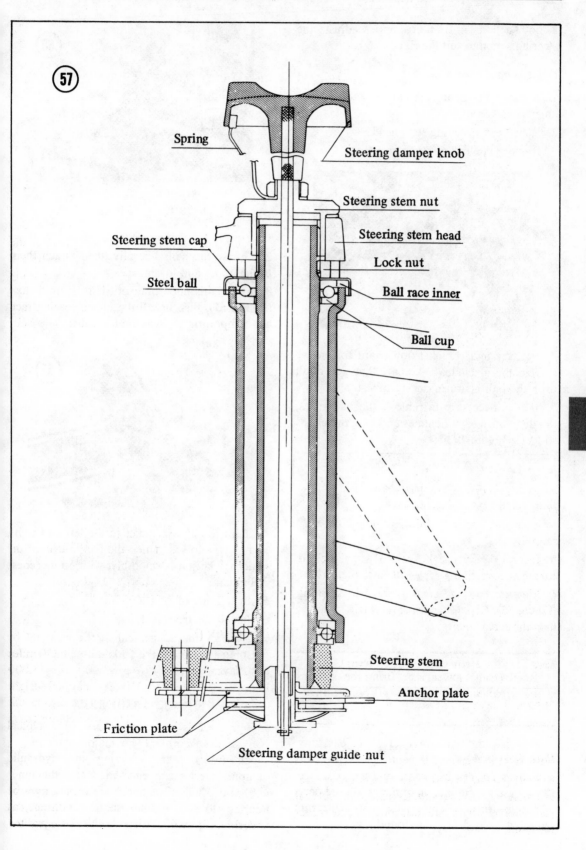

57

Spring

Steering damper knob

Steering stem nut

Steering stem head

Steering stem cap

Lock nut

Steel ball

Ball race inner

Ball cup

Steering stem

Anchor plate

Friction plate

Steering damper guide nut

smooth action. A friction damper adjusts the steering action to suit the rider.

Disassembly

1. Remove the handlebar, tachometer, speedometer, and front fork.
2. Remove the steering stem head.
3. Remove the lock nut (**Figure 58**).

4. Pull the underbracket downward to remove it from the machine. Take care that you don't drop the ball bearings during this step.
5. If it is necessary to remove the ball races, tap them out with a hammer and long punch, as shown in **Figure 59**.

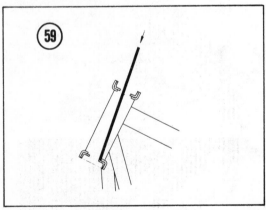

6. Remove the lower race from the steering stem with a hammer and chisel (**Figure 60**).

Inspection

Examine the underbracket shaft carefully. Replace it if the shaft is bent. Check the balls and races for cracks, wear, or other damage. Do not use a combination of new and used parts in the bearings. Replace the entire bearing assembly if any defects are found.

Reassembly

1. Press in the upper and lower races.
2. Grease the balls liberally, then attach them to the upper and lower races.
3. Insert the underbracket shaft from below (**Figure 61**), then install the upper bearing race and temporarily tighten the lock nut.

4. Turn the underbracket to the left and right, and as you do so, tighten the lock nut until the underbracket turns smoothly, with no looseness or binding.
5. Install the steering stem head.
6. Install the front fork legs.
7. Recheck the adjustment of the lock nut by grasping the tips of the forks and checking for any play.

SHOCK ABSORBERS

Figure 62 is a sectional view of a typical rear shock absorber. The major parts of the shock absorber are a spring and hydraulic damping mechanism encased within the inner and outer shells. The shock absorbers may be adjusted to suit various riding conditions, as shown in **Figure 63**. Adjust both sides equally.

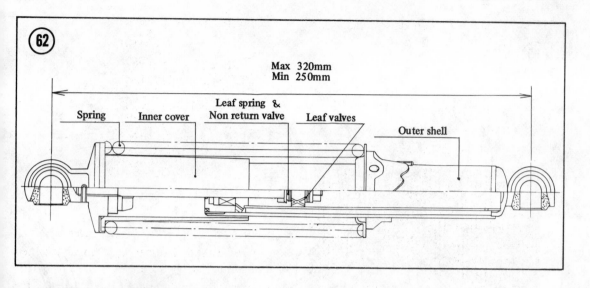

Max 320mm
Min 250mm

Spring Inner cover Leaf spring & Non return valve Leaf valves Outer shell

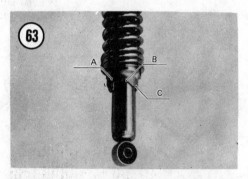

To remove the shock absorbers, remove the mounting bolts (**Figure 64**). Do not damage the rubber bushings as you remove and replace the bolts.

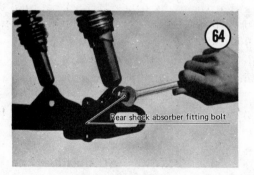

Rear shock absorber fitting bolt

Check the damping force by attempting to compress and extend the units quickly. If there is no marked difference between the effort required to operate the unit quickly or slowly, or if there are any oil leaks, replace the shock absorber.

FENDERS

Figure 65 (next page) illustrates typical fenders and their attaching parts. Front and rear fenders may be removed easily after the wheels are removed, merely by removing the attaching hardware (**Figures 66 and 67**).

SWINGING ARM

Figure 68 (p. 92) illustrates a typical swinging arm assembly. The entire assembly pivots up and down on the pivot shaft. The rear part of the

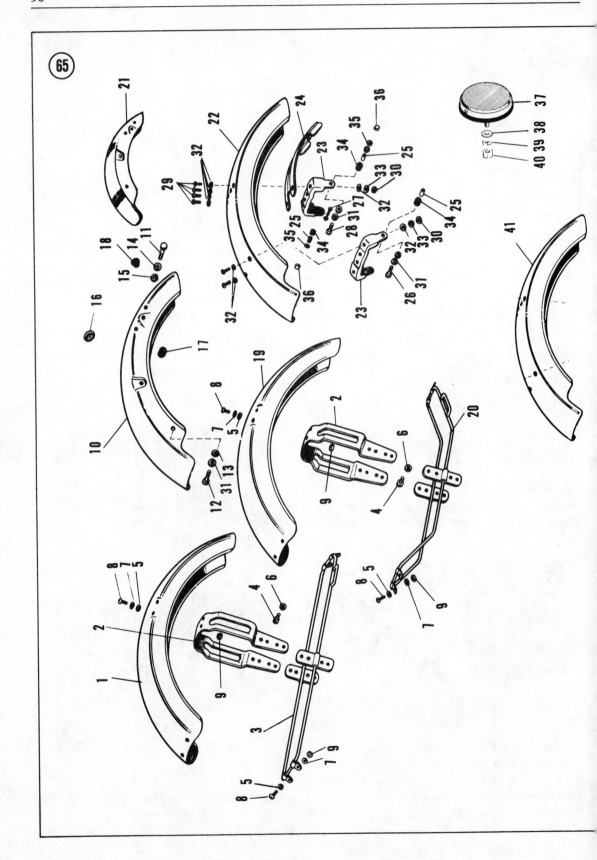

1. Front fender	22. Rear fender (stainless steel)
2. Fender brace	23. Fender bracket
3. Fender stay	24. Fender gusset
4. Hex bolt	25. Collar
5. Flat washer	26. Hex bolt
6. Lockwasher	27. Hex bolt
7. Lockwasher	28. Hex bolt
8. Pan head screw	29. Hex bolt
9. Hex nut	30. Hex nut
10. Rear fender	31. Lockwasher
11. Fender fitting bolt	32. Flat washer
12. Hex bolt	33. Lockwasher
13. Flat washer	34. Fuel tank shock damper
14. Lockwasher	35. Tank fitting washer
15. Flat washer	36. Tank fitting nut
16. Harness grommet	37. Reflector
17. Rubber plug	38. Flat washer
18. Fender plug	39. Lockwasher
19. Front fender	40. Nut
20. Fender stay	41. Rear fender (stainless steel)
21. Rear fender	

swinging arm is attached to the motorcycle frame through the shock absorbers.

Disassembly

1. Remove the drive chain.
2. Remove the rear sprocket (**Figure 69**).
3. Remove the pivot shaft (**Figure 70**).
4. Remove the swinging arm (**Figure 71**).

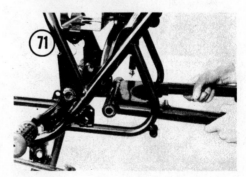

Inspection

The pivot section is susceptible to wear, especially in the bushings and shaft. Examine these parts carefully. Replace the pivot shaft if it is bent more than 0.02 inch (0.5 millimeter). Replace the bushings and/or the shaft if clearance between the shaft and the bushings exceeds

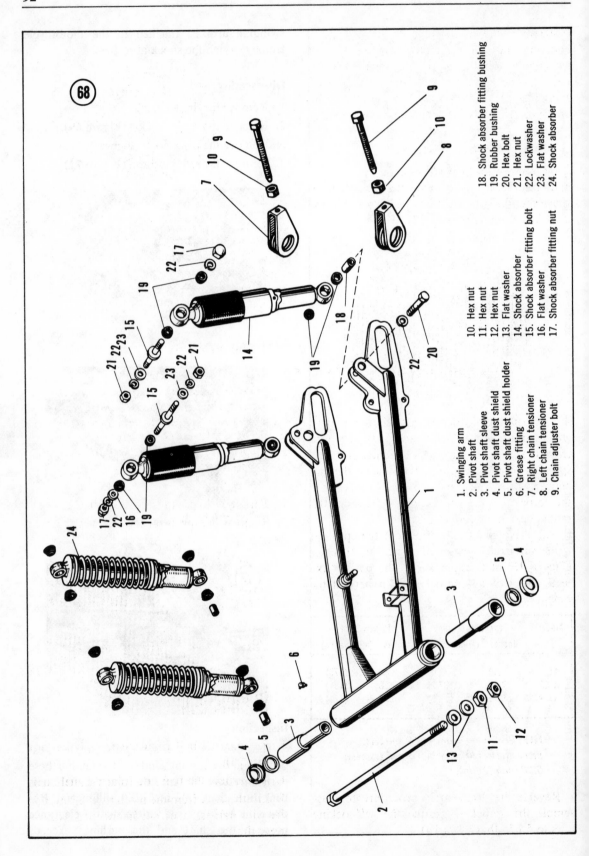

68

1. Swinging arm
2. Pivot shaft
3. Pivot shaft sleeve
4. Pivot shaft dust shield
5. Pivot shaft dust shield holder
6. Grease fitting
7. Right chain tensioner
8. Left chain tensioner
9. Chain adjuster bolt
10. Hex nut
11. Hex nut
12. Hex nut
13. Flat washer
14. Shock absorber
15. Shock absorber fitting bolt
16. Flat washer
17. Shock absorber fitting nut
18. Shock absorber fitting bushing
19. Rubber bushing
20. Hex bolt
21. Hex nut
22. Lockwasher
23. Flat washer
24. Shock absorber

0.008 inch (0.2 millimeter). Shimmy, wander, and wheel hop are common symptoms of worn swinging arm bushings. If either of the arms is bent, the rear wheel will be out of alignment. Examine the weld carefully. Replace the entire swinging arm assembly if the weld is cracked.

REAR SPROCKET

To remove the rear sprocket, use a hammer and chisel to remove the lockwashers, then remove the nuts which attach the sprocket to the sprocket coupling (**Figure 72**).

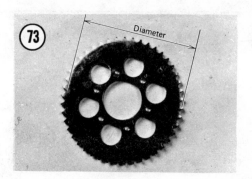

Any bending of the sprocket will make drive chain adjustment difficult, and may result in chain breakage. To check for bending, place the sprocket on a flat surface, then check the gap between the surface and the sprocket. Replace the sprocket if the gap exceeds 0.02 inch (0.5 millimeter) at any point.

The drive chain may slip from the sprocket if the sprocket is worn. Measure the diameter (**Figure 73**) of the sprocket at the base of the teeth. Replace any sprocket worn beyond the repair limit.

Model	Standard Value		Repair Limit	
	Inches	(Millimeters)	Inches	(Millimeters)
A1	7.0	(177.0)	6.88	(175)
A1SS	7.36	(187.1)	7.28	(185)
A7, A7SS	6.76	(171.9)	6.68	(170)

NOTE: *On A1R and A7R models, replace the sprocket when wear exceeds 0.08 inch (2mm).*

Reverse the disassembly procedure to reassemble the sprocket. Torque the self-locking nuts to 55 ft.-lb. (7.5 m-kg).

FUEL AND OIL TANKS

Figure 74 (next page) illustrates a typical fuel tank. The tank is made from corrosion resistant steel. A fuel cock is attached to the lower portion of the tank so that the fuel may be shut off when the machine is not running.

Fuel Tank Removal

WARNING
These operations, or any other operations which may result in spilled gasoline are potentially hazardous. Do not smoke or permit any sparks or open flame within 50 feet of your work area.

1. Turn the fuel cock to "0" (STOP).
2. Remove the nut from the front of the tank (**Figure 75**).

3. Remove the bolt from the rear of the tank (**Figure 76**).
4. Disconnect the fuel line from the fuel cock.
5. Lift the tank from the machine. Be sure that the wire harness does not interfere as you remove the tank.

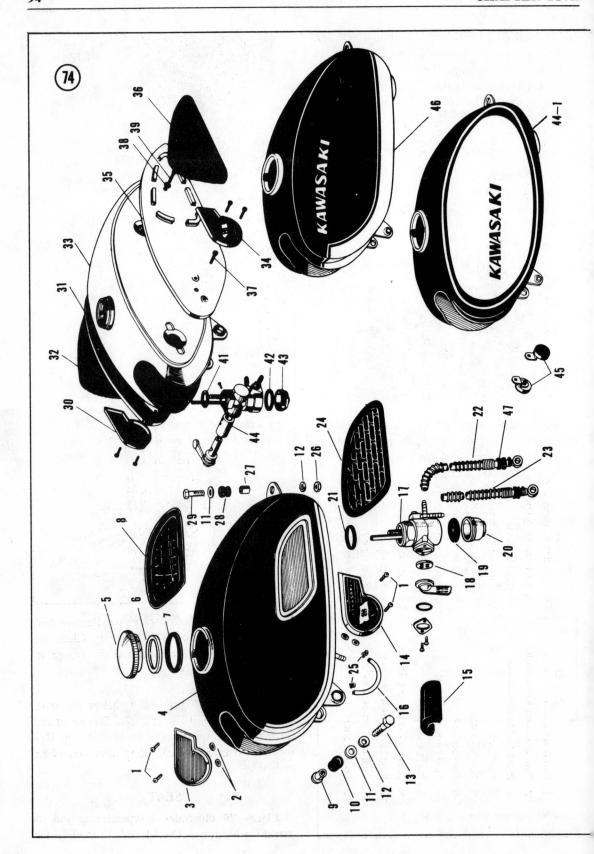

1. Pan head screw
2. Fuel tank emblem damper
3. Right fuel tank emblem
4. Fuel tank
5. Fuel tank cap
6. Fuel tank cap seal
7. Fuel tank cap gasket
8. Right knee grip
9. Fuel tank mounting spacer
10. Fuel tank shock damper
11. Fuel tank fitting washer
12. Lockwasher
13. Handlebar fitting bolt
14. Left fuel tank emblem
15. Fuel tank mat
16. Fuel tank connecting pipe
17. Fuel stranier body
18. Fuel strainer lever gasket
19. Fuel strainer cup gasket
20. Fuel strainer cup
21. Fuel strainer gasket
22. Fuel pipe B
23. Fuel pipe A
24. Left knee grip
25. Fuel tank connecting pipe clamp
26. Hex nut
27. Fuel tank mounting spacer
28. Fuel tank shock damper
29. Hex bolt
30. Right fuel tank emblem
31. Right fuel tank side panel
32. Right knee grip
33. Fuel tank
34. Left fuel tank emblem
35. Left fuel tank side panel
36. Left knee grip
37. Countersunk screw
38. Flat washer
39. Pan head screw
41. Fuel strainer gasket
42. Fuel strainer cup gasket
43. Fuel srtainer cup
44. Fuel strainer lever sleeve
44-1. Fuel tank
45. Reflector
46. Fuel tank
47. Pipe grommet

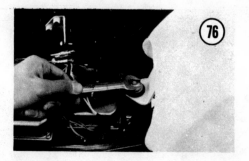

Fuel Cock

Figure 77 is a sectional view of a typical fuel cock. During normal running, fuel is drawn from the main standpipe within the fuel tank, which permits fuel to flow only as long as the fuel level remains above the top of the standpipe. Reserve fuel is supplied from the auxiliary standpipe.

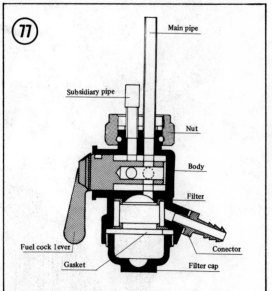

Inspect the fuel cock for leakage. Remove and clean the sediment bowl occasionally. Clean the fuel cock by blowing compressed air through it.

Oil Tank

The oil tank (**Figure 78**) is below the seat, on the right side of the machine. Service of the oil tank is limited to occasional cleaning. Remember to bleed the oil pump after you clean the tank.

SEAT

Figure 79 illustrates a typical seat and its attaching hardware. On A1 and A7 models, the

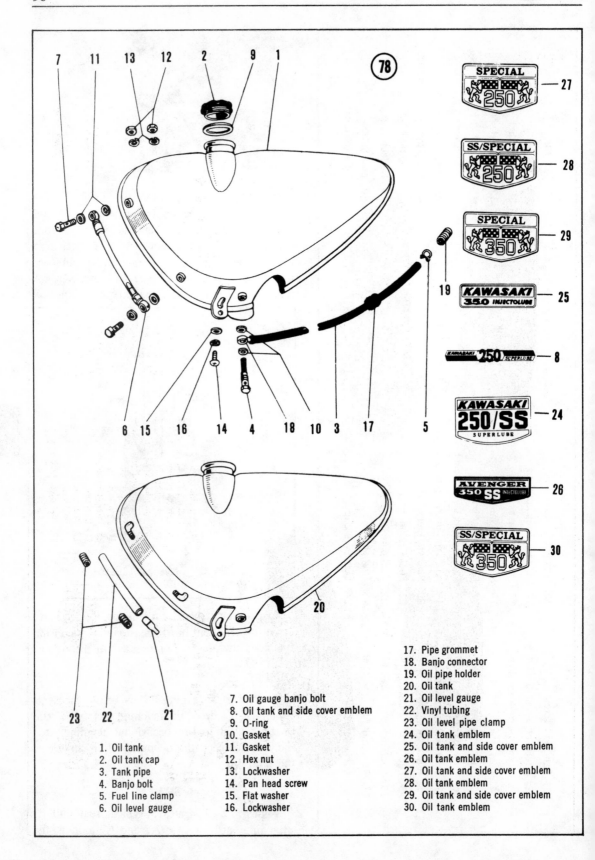

1. Oil tank
2. Oil tank cap
3. Tank pipe
4. Banjo bolt
5. Fuel line clamp
6. Oil level gauge
7. Oil gauge banjo bolt
8. Oil tank and side cover emblem
9. O-ring
10. Gasket
11. Gasket
12. Hex nut
13. Lockwasher
14. Pan head screw
15. Flat washer
16. Lockwasher
17. Pipe grommet
18. Banjo connector
19. Oil pipe holder
20. Oil tank
21. Oil level gauge
22. Vinyl tubing
23. Oil level pipe clamp
24. Oil tank emblem
25. Oil tank and side cover emblem
26. Oil tank emblem
27. Oil tank and side cover emblem
28. Oil tank emblem
29. Oil tank and side cover emblem
30. Oil tank emblem

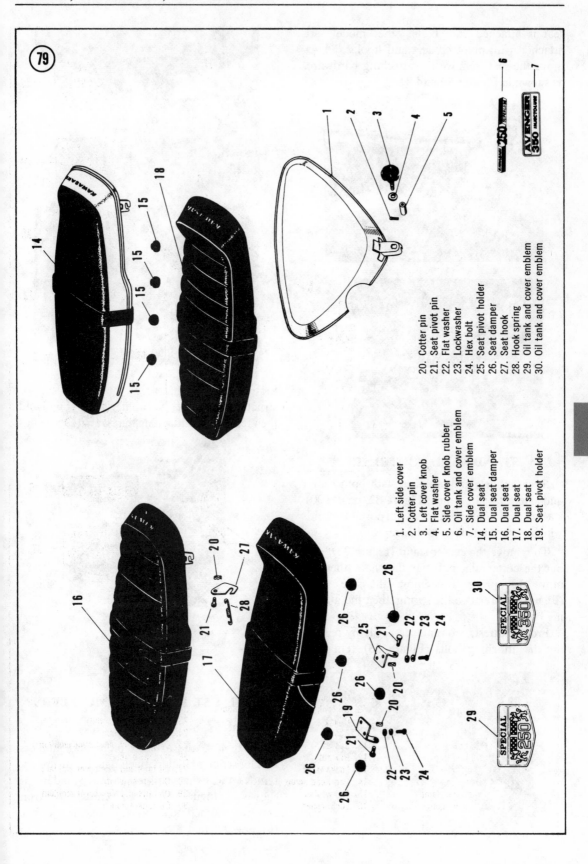

79

1. Left side cover
2. Cotter pin
3. Left cover knob
4. Flat washer
5. Side cover knob rubber
6. Oil tank and cover emblem
7. Side cover emblem
14. Dual seat
15. Dual seat
16. Dual seat
17. Dual seat
18. Dual seat
19. Seat pivot holder

20. Cotter pin
21. Seat pivot pin
22. Flat washer
23. Lockwasher
24. Hex bolt
25. Seat pivot holder
26. Seat damper
27. Seat hook
28. Hook spring
29. Oil tank and cover emblem
30. Oil tank and cover emblem

5

seat is attached with bolts; other models are attached with pivot holders and hooks. To remove the seat, remove the attaching hardware, as shown in **Figures 80 and 81**.

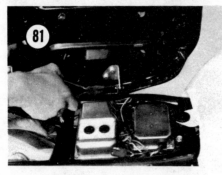

STANDS AND FOOTRESTS

Street models are equipped with both center and side, or kick, stands (**Figure 82**, page 100). Racing models are equipped with portable stands which are not attached to the frame.

To remove the center stand (**Figure 83**), pull out the cotter pin, pull out the shaft, then remove the spring. To remove the side stand (**Figure 84**), remove the spring, then the attaching bolt.

Front footrests are removed easily by removing the attaching bolts (**Figure 85**). The rear

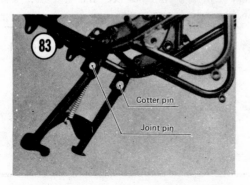
Cotter pin
Joint pin

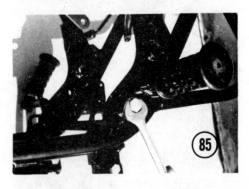

footrests are extensions of the muffler support structure. Support the muffler with your hand, then remove the attaching hardware (**Figure 86**).

EXHAUST PIPES AND MUFFLERS

Removal

To remove the exhaust pipes and mufflers, first loosen the muffler attachment hardware and remove the exhaust pipes at the cylinders, as shown in **Figure 87**. Then remove the front and rear attachment bolts from the mufflers (**Figures 88 and 89**).

To remove the baffle tube, remove the screw at the back of the muffler (**Figure 90**), then pull out the baffle tube (**Figure 91**).

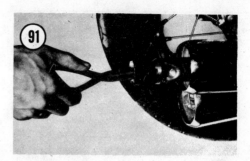

Inspection

Carbon deposits within the exhaust pipe and muffler cause the engine to lose power. Clean the carbon from the baffle tube with a wire brush. If the deposits are too heavy to remove with a brush, heat the baffle tube with a torch (**Figure 92**) and tap the tube lightly. Clean carbon deposits from the exhaust pipe by running a used drive chain through the pipe.

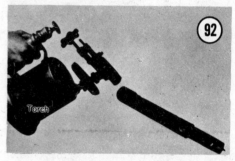

As the machine ages, the joint between the exhaust pipe and muffler may leak. Replace the rubber connector if leakage occurs.

Always use new gaskets upon reassembly.

DRIVE CHAIN

The drive chain (**Figure 93**) becomes worn after prolonged use. Wear in the pins, bushings, and rollers causes the chain to stretch. Sliding between the roller surface and sprocket teeth also contributes to wear.

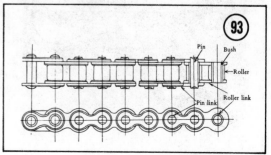

5

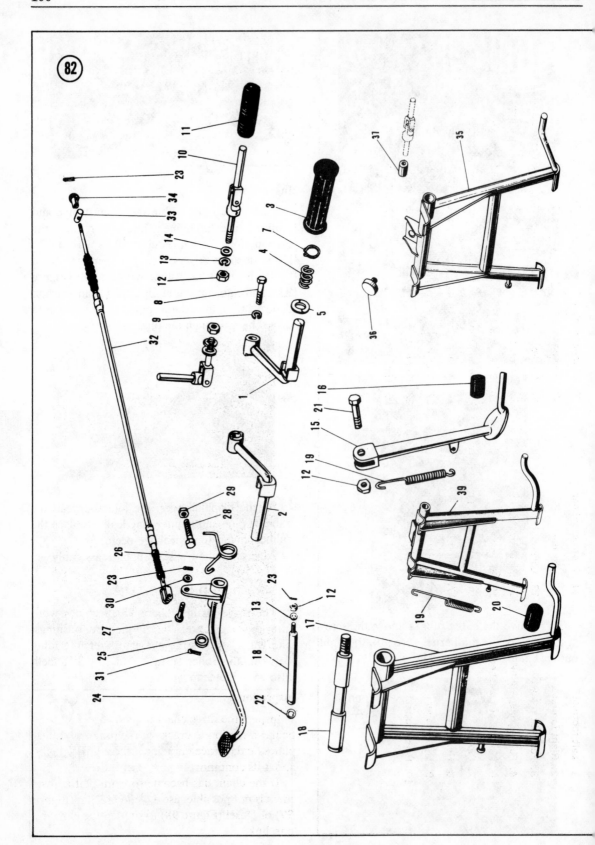

1. Left footrest
2. Right footrest
3. Footrest rubber
4. Folding peg spring
5. Folding peg washer
7. Circlip
8. Hex bolt
9. Lockwasher
10. Rear footrest

11. Footrest rubber
12. Hex nut
13. Lockwasher
14. Flat washer
15. Kickstand
16. Kickstand stopper rubber
17. Center stand
18. Center stand shaft
19. Stand spring

20. Stopper rubber
21. Hex bolt
22. Circlip
23. Cotter pin
24. Brake pedal
25. Pedal fitting washer
26. Pedal return spring
27. Rear brake cable joint pin
28. Hex bolt
29. Hex nut

30. Flat washer
31. Cotter pin
32. Rear brake cable
33. Brake cable joint
34. Cable adjusting nut
35. Center stand
36. Center stand stopper rubber
37. Footrest bar collar
39. Center stand

Adjust the free play in the chain so that there is one inch (25 millimeters) vertical play (**Figure 94**) in the center of the chain run with the machine on the ground. **Figure 95** illustrates the adjustment procedure. Be sure to adjust each side equally. The rear brake is affected by any chain adjustment. Be sure to adjust the rear brake after you adjust the chain (**Figure 96**).

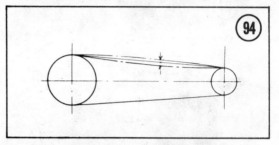

Inspection

Inspect the drive chain periodically. Pay particular attention to cracks in the rollers and link plates, and replace the chain if there is any doubt about its condition.

If the chain has become so worn that adjustment is not possible, use a chain breaker (**Figure 97**) or chisel (**Figure 98**) to shorten the chain by one link.

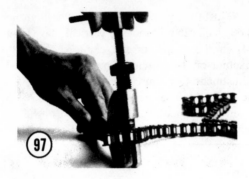

As the steering stem moves, the damper piston moves back and forth within the damper cylinder. As the piston moves, oil is forced through a small orifice in the piston, thereby preventing rapid motion of the steering stem.

To remove the oil damper, remove the attaching hardware (**Figure 101**).

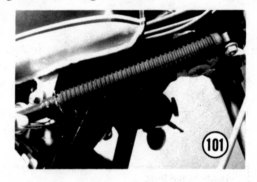

Install the master link so that the clip opening faces opposite to the direction of chain movement (**Figure 99**). Failure to do so may result in loss of the clip and resultant chain breakage.

HYDRAULIC STEERING DAMPER

The hydraulic steering damper is connected between the frame and steering head. The damper absorbs handlebar vibration during high speed riding. **Figure 100** is a cutaway view of the damper.

Check the condition of the damper by alternately compressing and extending it quickly. If little or no resistance is encountered as you operate it, or if any oil leakage is evident, replace it. The steering oil damper is not serviceable.

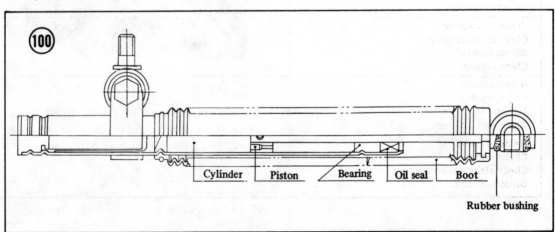

Cylinder   Piston   Bearing   Oil seal   Boot

Rubber bushing

CHAPTER SIX

PERIODIC SERVICE AND MAINTENANCE

To gain the utmost in safety, performance, and useful life from your machine, it is necessary to make periodic inspections and adjustments. It frequently happens that minor problems are found during such inspections that are simple and inexpensive to correct at the time, but which could lead to major problems later.

The following table is a suggested maintenance schedule. The procedures for performing these services are described in the applicable chapters.

Maintenance Item	Miles		
	Initial 500	1,000	2,000
Change oil	X		X
Check spark plugs	X		X
Ignition timing	X		X
Adjust clutch	X		X
Adjust carburetors	X		X
Adjust oil pump	X		X
Clean air cleaner			X
Clean exhaust system			X
Adjust brakes	X	X	
Clean brakes		X	
Inspect chain	X		X
Check spokes		X	
Tighten all fastenings	X		X
Clean fuel strainer		X	
Remove carbon			X
Check battery	X	X	
Check electrical equipment	X	X	
Grease chassis		X	

CHAPTER SEVEN

TROUBLESHOOTING

Diagnosing motorcycle ills is relatively simple if you use orderly procedures and keep a few basic principles in mind.

Never assume anything. Don't overlook the obvious. If you are riding along and the bike suddenly quits, check the easiest, most accessible problem spots first. Is there gasoline in the tank? Is the gas petcock in the "on" or "reserve" position? Has a spark plug wire fallen off? Check the ignition switch. Sometimes the weight of keys on a key ring may turn the ignition off suddenly.

If nothing obvious turns up in a cursory check, look a little further. Learning to recognize and describe symptoms will make repairs easier for you or a mechanic at the shop. Describe problems accurately and fully. Saying that "it won't run" isn't the same as saying "it quit on the highway at high speed and wouldn't start," or that "it sat in my garage for three months and then wouldn't start."

Gather as many symptoms together as possible to aid in diagnosis. Note whether the engine lost power gradually or all at once, what color smoke (if any) came from the exhausts and so on. Remember that the more complicated a machine is, the easier it is to troubleshoot because symptoms point to specific problems.

You don't need fancy equipment or complicated test gear to determine whether repairs can be attempted at home. A few simple checks could save a large repair bill and time lost while the bike sits in a dealer's service department. On the other hand, be realistic and don't attempt repairs beyond your abilities. Service departments tend to charge heavily for putting together a disassembled engine that may have been abused. Some won't even take on such a job—so use common sense; don't get in over your head.

OPERATING REQUIREMENTS

An engine needs three basics to run properly: correct gas/air mixture, compression, and a spark at the right time. If one or more are missing, the engine won't run. The electrical system is the weakest link of the three. More problems result from electrical breakdowns than from any other source. Keep that in mind before you begin tampering with carburetor adjustments and the like.

If a bike has been sitting for any length of time and refuses to start, check the battery for a charged condition first, and then look to the gasoline delivery system. This includes the tank, fuel petcocks, lines, and the carburetor. Rust may have formed in the tank, obstructing fuel flow. Gasoline deposits may have gummed up carburetor jets and air passages. Gasoline tends to lose its potency after standing for long periods. Condensation may contaminate it with water. Drain old gas and try starting with a fresh tankful.

Compression or the lack of it, usually enters the picture only in the case of older machines. Worn or broken pistons, rings, and cylinder bores could prevent starting. Generally a gradual power loss and harder and harder starting will be readily apparent in this case.

STARTING DIFFICULTIES

Check gas flow first. Remove the gas cap and look into the tank. If gas is present, pull off a fuel line at the carburetor and see if gas flows freely. If none comes out, the fuel tap may be shut off, blocked by rust or foreign matter, or the fuel line may be stopped up or kinked. If the carburetor is getting usable fuel, turn to the electrical system next.

Check that the battery is charged by turning on the lights or by beeping the horn. Refer to your owner's manual for starting procedures with a dead battery. Have the battery recharged if necessary.

Pull off a spark plug cap, remove the spark plug, and reconnect the cap. Lay the plug against the cylinder head so its base makes a good connection, and turn the engine over with the kickstarter. A fat, blue spark should jump across the electrodes. If there is no spark, or only a weak one, there is electrical system trouble. Check for a defective plug by replacing it with a known good one. Don't assume a plug is good just because it's new.

Once the plug has been cleared of guilt, but there's still no spark, start backtracking through the system. If the contact at the end of the spark plug wire can be exposed, it can be held about ⅛ inch from the head while the engine is turned over to check for a spark. Remember to hold the wire only by its insulation to avoid a nasty shock. If the plug wires are dirty, greasy, or wet, wrap a rag around them so you don't get shocked. If you do feel a shock or see sparks along the wire, clean or replace the wire and/or its connections.

If there's no spark at the plug wire, look for loose connections at the coil and battery. If all seems in order here, check next for oily or dirty contact points. Clean points with electrical contact cleaner, or a strip of paper. On battery ignition models, turn the switch on, then open and close the points manually with a screwdriver.

No spark at the points with this test indicates a failure in the ignition system. Refer to Chapter Three (Electrical System) for checkout procedures for the entire system and individual components. Refer to the same chapter for checking and setting ignition timing.

Note that spark plugs of the incorrect heat range (too cold) may cause hard starting. Set gaps to specifications. If you have just ridden through a puddle or washed the bike and it won't start, dry off plugs and plug wires. Water may have entered the carburetor and fouled the fuel under these conditions, but wet plugs and wires are the more likely problem.

If a healthy spark occurs at the right time, and there is adequate gas flow to the carburetor, check the carburetor itself at this time. Make sure all jets and air passages are clean, check float level, and adjust if necessary. Shake the float to check for gasoline inside it, and replace or repair as indicated. Check that the carburetors are mounted snugly, and no air is leaking past the manifold. Check for a clogged air filter.

Compression may be checked in the field by turning the kickstarter by hand and noting that an adequate resistance is felt, or by removing a spark plug and placing a finger over the plug hole and feeling for pressure.

An accurate compression check gives a good idea of the condition of the basic working parts of the engine. To perform this test, you need a compression gauge. The motor should be warm.

1. Remove the plug on the cylinder to be tested and clean out any dirt or grease.

2. Insert the tip of the gauge into the hole, making sure it is seated correctly.

3. Open the throttle all the way and make sure the chokes on the carburetors are open.

4. Crank the engine several times and record the highest pressure reading on the gauge. Run the test on each of the cylinders. Refer to Chapter Two (Engine, Transmission, and Clutch) to interpret results.

POOR IDLING

Poor idling may be caused by incorrect carburetor adjustment, incorrect timing, or ignition system defects. Check the gas cap vent for an obstruction.

MISFIRING

Misfiring can be caused by a weak spark or dirty plugs. Check for fuel contamination. Run the machine at night or in a darkened garage to check for spark leaks along the plug wires and under the spark plug cap. If misfiring occurs only at certain throttle settings, refer to the carburetor chapter for the specific carburetor circuits involved. Misfiring under heavy load, as when climbing hills or accelerating, is usually caused by bad spark plugs.

FLAT SPOTS

If the engine seems to die momentarily when the throttle is opened and then recovers, check for a dirty main jet in the carburetor, water in the fuel, or an excessively lean mixture.

POWER LOSS

Poor condition of rings, pistons, or cylinders will cause a lack of power and speed. Ignition timing should be checked.

OVERHEATING

If the engine seems to run too hot all the time, be sure you are not idling it for long periods. Air-cooled engines are not designed to operate at a standstill for any length of time. Heavy stop and go traffic is hard on a motorcycle engine. Spark plugs of the wrong heat range can burn pistons. An excessively lean gas mixture may cause overheating. Check ignition timing. Don't ride in too high a gear. Broken or worn rings may permit compression gases to leak past them, heating heads and cylinders excessively. Check oil level and use the proper grade lubricants.

BACKFIRING

Check that the timing is not advanced too far. Check fuel for contamination.

ENGINE NOISES

Experience is needed to diagnose accurately in this area. Noises are hard to differentiate and harder yet to describe. Deep knocking noises uually mean main bearing failure. A slapping noise generally comes from loose pistons. A light knocking noise during acceleration may be a bad connecting rod bearing. Pinging, which sounds like marbles being shaken in a tin can, is caused by ignition advanced too far or gasoline with too low an octane rating. Pinging should be corrected immediately or damage to pistons will result. Compression leaks at the head-cylinder joint will sound like a rapid on and off squeal.

PISTON SEIZURE

Piston seizure is caused by incorrect piston clearances when fitted, fitting rings with improper end gap, too thin an oil being used, incorrect spark plug heat range, or incorrect ignition timing. Overheating from any cause may result in seizure.

EXCESSIVE VIBRATION

Excessive vibration may be caused by loose motor mounts, worn engine or transmission bearings, loose wheels, worn swinging arm bushings, a generally poor running engine, broken or cracked frame, or one that has been damaged in a collision. See also Poor Handling.

CLUTCH SLIP OR DRAG

Clutch slip may be due to worn plates, improper adjustment, or glazed plates. A dragging clutch could result from damaged or bent plates, improper adjustment, or even clutch spring pressure.

POOR HANDLING

Poor handling may be caused by improper tire pressures, a damaged frame or swinging arm, worn shocks or front forks, weak fork springs, a bent or broken steering stem, misaligned wheels, loose or missing spokes, worn tires, bent handlebars, worn wheel bearing, or dragging brakes.

BRAKE PROBLEMS

Sticking brakes may be caused by broken or weak return springs, improper cable or rod adjustment, or dry pivot and cam bushings. Grabbing brakes may be caused by greasy linings which must be replaced. Brake grab may also be due to out-of-round drums or linings which have broken loose from the brake shoes. Glazed linings or glazed brake pads will cause loss of stopping power.

LIGHTING PROBLEMS

Bulbs which continuously burn out may be caused by excessive vibration, loose connections that permit sudden current surges, poor battery connections, or installation of the wrong type bulb.

A dead battery or one which discharges quickly may be caused by a faulty generator or rectifier. Check for loose or corroded terminals. Shorted battery cells or broken terminals will keep a battery from charging. Low water level will decrease a battery's capacity. A battery left uncharged after installation will sulphate, rendering it useless.

A majority of light and horn or other electrical accessory problems are caused by loose or corroded ground connections. Check those first, and then substitute known good units for easier troubleshooting.

TROUBLESHOOTING GUIDE

The following "quick reference" guide summarizes the troubleshooting process. Use it to outline possible problem areas, then refer to the specific chapter or section involved.

LOSS OF POWER

Cause	Things to check	Cause	Things to check
Poor compression	Piston rings and cylinders Head gaskets Crankcase leaks	Improper mixture	Dirty air cleaner Starter lever position Restricted fuel flow Gas cap vent hole
Overheated engine	Lubricating oil supply Oil pump Clogged cooling fins Ignition timing Slipping clutch Carbon in combustion chamber	Miscellaneous	Dragging brakes Tight wheel bearings Defective chain Clogged exhaust system

STEERING PROBLEMS

Problem	Things to check	Problem	Things to check
Hard steering	Tire pressures Steering damper adjustment Steering stem head Steering head bearings Steering oil damper	Pulls to one side	Defective swinging arm Defective steering head Defective steering oil damper
Pulls to one side	Unbalanced shock absorbers Drive chain adjustment Front/rear wheel alignment Unbalanced tires	Shimmy	Drive chain adjustment Loose or missing spokes Deformed rims Worn wheel bearings Wheel balance

7

GEARSHIFTING DIFFICULTIES

Cause	Things to check	Cause	Things to check
Clutch	Adjustment Springs Friction plates Steel plates	Transmission	Return spring or pin Change lever or spring Drum lever or lever spring Drum position plate Change drum Change forks
Transmission	Oil quantity Oil grade		

BRAKE TROUBLES

Problem	Things to check	Problem	Things to check
Poor brakes	Brake adjustment Oil or water on brake linings Loose linkage or cables	Unadjustable brakes	Worn linings Worn drums Worn brake cams
Noisy brakes	Worn or scratched lining Scratched brake drums Dirt in brakes		

CHAPTER EIGHT

SPECIFICATIONS

This chapter contains specifications and performance figures for the various Kawasaki models covered by this book. The tables are arranged in order of increasing engine size. Since there are differences between various models of the same engine size, be sure to consult the correct table for the motorcycle in question.

SPECIFICATIONS, MODEL A1

DIMENSIONS
Overall Length	78.3 in.
Overall Width	31.9 in.
Overall Height	43.1 in.
Wheelbase	51.2 in.
Road Clearance	6.5 in.
Dry Weight	318.5 lb.

PERFORMANCE
Maximum Speed	103 mph
Fuel Consumption	80 mpg
Climbing Ability	38°
Braking Distance	39 ft/31 mph
Minimum Turning Radius	86.6 in.

ENGINE
Type	2-cycle, 2 cylinder
Bore x Stroke	2.09 x 2.21 in.
Displacement	15.07 cu. in. (247cc)
Compression Ratio	7.0:1
Maximum Horsepower	31 hp/8,000 rpm
Maximum Torque ft-lb/rpm	2.92/7,500

VALVE TIMING
Inlet		
Open BTC	112°	
Close ATC	65°	
Scavenging		
Open BBC	58°	
Close ABC	58°	
Exhaust		
Open BBC	89°	
Close ABC	89°	
Carburetor Type	(2) VM22SC	
Fuel Tank Capacity	3.5 gal.	
Lubrication System	Superlube Oil Injection	
Engine Oil	2-stroke engine oil	
Oil Tank Capacity	2.4 qt.	
Starting System	Kickstarter	
Ignition System	Battery and Coil	
Ignition Type	Conventional/C.D.I.	
Ignition Timing (before TDC)	23°	25°

(continued)

SPECIFICATIONS, MODEL A1 (continued)		
SPARK PLUG		
NGK	B-9HC	—
Hitachi	—	—
Denso	—	—
Champion	L-60T	UL-19V
Autolite	—	—
Bosch	W340T16	—
KLG	F290	
Lodge	R-50	
TRANSMISSION		
Type	5-speed, constant mesh, return change	
GEAR RATIO		
Low	2.50	
2nd	1.53	
3rd	1.13	
4th	0.92	
5th	0.78	
Primary Reduction Ratio	3.40 (51/15)	
Final Reduction Ratio	2.46 (37/15)	
Overall Drive Ratio	6.52	
Transmission Oil	SAE 30	
Transmission Oil Capacity	1.27 qt.	
CLUTCH		
Type	Heavy duty multiple disk, Wet plate	
ELECTRICAL EQUIPMENT		
Generator		
Made by	Kokusan	Mitsubishi
Type	EN10	AW2010A
Regulator		
Made by	Kokusan	Mitsubishi
Type	ZR 905	RL2128T
Ignition Coil		
Made by	Diamond	Diamond
Type	TU-25M-7	TU-51-1
Battery		
Type	12N614A	
Capacity	12V6AH	

8

(continued)

SPECIFICATIONS, MODEL A1 (continued)

ELECTRICAL EQUIPMENT (continued)
Head Lamp Type	Semi-sealed beam
Head Lamp	12V, 35/25W
Tail/Brake Lamp	12V, 8/25W (4/32 cp)
Speedometer Lamp	12V, 3W
Neutral Indicator	12V, 3W
Tachometer Indicator Lamp Bulb	12V, 3W
Charge Indicator Lamp Bulb	— —
High Beam Indicator Bulb	12V, 1.5W
Turn Signal Lamp Bulb	12V, 8W

FRAME
Type	Tubular, double cradle
Steering Angle	40°
Caster	63°
Trail	3.4 in.
Tire Size	
Front	3.00-18, 4PR
Rear	3.25-18, 4PR
Suspension	
Front	Telescopic Fork
Rear	Swinging Arm
Damper Stroke	
Front	4.3 in.
Rear	2.8 in.
Front Fork Oil Capacity	
(each fork)	0.22 qt.
Mixing Ratio	
Mobil Oil	
Spindle Oil	8:2
Diameter x Width	
Front	7.1 x 1.2 in.
Rear	7.1 x 1.2 in.

SPECIFICATIONS, MODEL A1SS		
DIMENSIONS		
Overall Length	78.3 in.	
Overall Width	32.6 in.	
Overall Height	42.5 in.	
Wheelbase	51.0 in.	
Road Clearance	6.7 in.	
Dry Weight	323.3 lb.	
PERFORMANCE		
Maximum Speed	103 mph	
Fuel Consumption	80 mpg	
Climbing Ability	39°	
Braking Distance	39 ft/31 mph	
Minimum Turning Radius	86.6 in.	
ENGINE		
Type	2-cycle, 2 cylinder	
Bore x Stroke	2.09 x 2.21 in.	
Displacement	15.07 cu. in. (247cc)	
Compression Ratio	7.0:1	
Maximum Horsepower	31 hp/8,000 rpm	
Maximum Torque ft-lb/rpm	2.92/7,500	
VALVE TIMING		
Inlet		
Open BTC	112°	
Close ATC	65°	
Scavenging		
Open BBC	58°	
Close ABC	58°	
Exhaust		
Open BBC	89°	
Close ABC	89°	
Carburetor Type	(2) VM22SC	
Fuel Tank Capacity	3.5 gal.	
Lubrication System	Superlube Oil Injection	
Engine Oil	2-stroke engine oil	
Oil Tank Capacity	2.4 qt.	
Starting System	Kickstarter	
Ignition System	Battery and Coil	
Ignition Type	Conventional/C.D.I.	
Ignition Timing (before TDC)	23°	25°

(continued)

8

SPECIFICATIONS, MODEL A1SS (continued)

SPARK PLUG
NGK	B-9HC	—
Hitachi	—	—
Denso	—	—
Champion	L-60T	UL019V
Autolite	—	—
Bosch	W340T16	—
KLG	F290	—
Lodge	R-50	—

TRANSMISSION
Type	5-speed, constant mesh, return change

GEAR RATIO
Low	2.50
2nd	1.53
3rd	1.13
4th	0.92
5th	0.78
Primary Reduction Ratio	3.40 (51/15)
Final Reduction Ratio	2.60 (39/15)
Overall Drive Ratio	6.89
Transmission Oil	SAE 30
Transmission Oil Capacity	1.27 qt.

CLUTCH
Type	Heavy duty multiple disk, Wet plate

ELECTRICAL EQUIPMENT
Generator		
Made by	Kokusan	Mitsubishi
Type	EN10	AW2010A
Regulator		
Made by	Kokusan	Mitsubishi
Type	ZR 905	RL2128T
Ignition Coil		
Made by	Diamond	Diamond
Type	TU-25M-7	TU-51-1
Battery		
Type	12N6-4A	
Capacity	12V6AH	

(continued)

SPECIFICATIONS, MODEL A1SS (continued)	
ELECTRICAL EQUIPMENT (continued)	
Head Lamp Type	Semi-sealed beam
Head Lamp	12V, 35/25W
Tail/Brake Lamp	12V, 8/25W (4/32 cp)
Speedometer Lamp	12V, 3W
Neutral Indicator	12V, 3W
Tachometer Indicator Lamp Bulb	12V, 3W
Charge Indicator Lamp Bulb	— —
High Beam Indicator Bulb	12V, 1.5W
Turn Signal Lamp Bulb	12V, 8W
FRAME	
Type	Tubular, double cradle
Steering Angle	40°
Caster	63°
Trail	3.4 in.
Tire Size	
Front	3.00-18, 4PR
Rear	3.50-18, 4PR
Suspension	
Front	Telescopic Fork
Rear	Swinging Arm
Damper Stroke	
Front	4.3 in.
Rear	2.8 in.
Front Fork Oil Capacity	
(each fork)	0.22 qt.
Mixing Ratio	
Mobil Oil	
Spindle Oil	8:2
Diameter x Width	
Front	7.1 x 1.2 in.
Rear	7.1 x 1.2 in.

8

SPECIFICATIONS, MODEL A1R	
DIMENSIONS	
Overall Length	75.4 in.
Overall Width	22.8 in.
Overall Height	37.2 in.
Wheelbase	51.0 in.
Road Clearance	4.9 in.
Dry Weight	239.7 lb.
PERFORMANCE	
Maximum Speed	125 mph
Fuel Consumption	—
Climbing Ability	—
Braking Distance	—
Minimum Turning Radius	150.0 in.
ENGINE	
Type	2-cycle, 2 cylinder
Bore x Stroke	2.09 x 2.21 in.
Displacement	15.07 cu. in. (247cc)
Compression Ratio	8.0:1
Maximum Horsepower	40 hp/9,500 rpm
Maximum Torque ft-lb/rpm	3.00/8,500
VALVE TIMING	
Inlet	
Open BTC	130°
Close ATC	70°
Scavenging	
Open BBC	62°
Close ABC	62°
Exhaust	
Open BBC	94.5°
Close ABC	94.5°
Carburetor Type	(2) M26R
Fuel Tank Capacity	5.3 gal.
Lubrication System	Superlube and Gasoline Oil
Engine Oil	(15:1) Mixing
Oil Tank Capacity	1.05 qt.
Starting System	Push or Kick
Ignition System	Magneto
Ignition Type	Conventional
Ignition Timing (before TDC)	23°

(continued)

SPECIFICATIONS, MODEL A1R (continued)	
SPARK PLUG	
NGK	B-10EN
Hitachi	—
Denso	—
Champion	L-55T
Autolite	AE-403
Bosch	W370T16
KLG	—
Lodge	—
TRANSMISSION	
Type	5-speed, constant mesh, return change
GEAR RATIO	
Low	2.06 (33/16)
2nd	1.47 (28/19)
3rd	1.18 (26/22)
4th	1.00 (24/24)
5th	0.89 (23/26)
Primary Reduction Ratio	3.35 (57/17)
Final Reduction Ratio	1.81 (29/16)
Overall Drive Ratio	5.38
Transmission Oil	SAE 10W30
Transmission Oil Capacity	1.27 qt.
CLUTCH	
Type	Heavy duty multiple disk, Wet plate
ELECTRICAL EQUIPMENT	
Generator	
Made by	Kokusan
Type	EN04
Regulator	
Made by	—
Type	
Ignition Coil	
Made by	Kokusan
Type	ST-70
Battery	
Type	—
Capacity	

(continued)

8

SPECIFICATIONS, MODEL A1R (continued)

FRAME
  Type   Tubular, double cradle
  Steering Angle   40°
  Caster   63°
  Trail   3.4 in.
  Tire Size
    Front   2.75-18, 4PR
    Rear   3.00-18, 4PR
  Suspension
    Front   Telescopic Fork
    Rear   Swinging Arm
  Damper Stroke
    Front   4.7 in.
    Rear   2.8 in.
  Front Fork Oil Capacity
    (each fork)   0.24 qt.
  Mixing Ratio
    Mobil Oil
    Spindle Oil   8:2
  Diameter x Width
    Front   7.9 x 0.8 in.
    Rear   7.1 x 1.4 in.

SPECIFICATIONS, MODEL A7	
DIMENSIONS	
Overall Length	79.0 in.
Overall Width	31.9 in.
Overall Height	43.5 in.
Wheelbase	51.0 in.
Road Clearance	6.7 in.
Dry Weight	327.7 lb.
PERFORMANCE	
Maximum Speed	110 mph
Fuel Consumption	80 mpg
Climbing Ability	40°
Braking Distance	39 ft/31 mph
Minimum Turning Radius	86.6 in.
ENGINE	
Type	2-cycle, 2 cylinder
Bore x Stroke	2.44 x 2.21 in.
Displacement	20.63 cu. in. (338cc)
Compression Ratio	7.0:1
Maximum Horsepower	42 hp/8,000 rpm
Maximum Torque ft-lb/rpm	3.99/7,000
VALVE TIMING	
Inlet	
Open BTC	112°
Close ATC	65°
Scavenging	
Open BBC	60°
Close ABC	60°
Exhaust	
Open BBC	91°
Close ABC	91°
Carburetor Type	(2) VM28SC
Fuel Tank Capacity	3.5 gal.
Lubrication System	Injecto lube Oil Injection
Engine Oil	2-stroke engine oil
Oil Tank Capacity	2.4 qt.
Starting System	Kickstarter
Ignition System	Battery and Coil
Ignition Type	Conventional/C.D.I.
Ignition Timing (before TDC)	23° 25°

8

(continued)

SPECIFICATIONS, MODEL A7 (continued)

SPARK PLUG		
NGK	B-9HC	—
Hitachi	—	—
Denso	—	—
Champion	L-60T	UL-19V
Autolite	—	—
Bosch	W340T16	—
KLG	F290	—
Lodge	R-50	—

TRANSMISSION	
Type	5-speed, constant mesh, return change

GEAR RATIO	
Low	2.50
2nd	1.53
3rd	1.13
4th	0.92
5th	0.78
Primary Reduction Ratio	3.40 (51/15)
Final Reduction Ratio	2.40 (36/15)
Overall Drive Ratio	6.36
Transmission Oil	SAE 30
Transmission Oil Capacity	1.27 qt.

CLUTCH	
Type	Heavy duty multiple disk, Wet plate

ELECTRICAL EQUIPMENT		
Generator		
Made by	Kokusan	Mitsubishi
Type	EN8	AW2010A
Regulator		
Made by	Kokusan	Mitsubishi
Type	ZR906	RL2128T
Ignition Coil		
Made by	Diamond	Diamond
Type	TU-25M-7	TU-51-1
Battery		
Type	12N 6-4A	
Capacity	12V 6AH	

(continued)

SPECIFICATIONS, MODEL A7 (continued)

ELECTRICAL EQUIPMENT (continued)

Head Lamp Type	Semi-sealed beam
Head Lamp	12V, 35/25W
Tail/Brake Lamp	12V, 8/25W (4/32 cp)
Speedometer Lamp	12V, 3W
Neutral Indicator	12V, 3W
Tachometer Indicator Lamp Bulb	12V, 3W
Charge Indicator Lamp Bulb	— —
High Beam Indicator Bulb	
Turn Signal Lamp Bulb	12V, 8W

FRAME

Type	Tubular, double cradle
Steering Angle	40°
Caster	63°
Trail	3.6 in.
Tire Size	
Front	3.25-18, 4PR
Rear	3.50-18, 4PR
Suspension	
Front	Telescopic Fork
Rear	Swinging Arm
Damper Stroke	
Front	4.3 in.
Rear	2.8 in.
Front Fork Oil Capacity	
(each fork)	0.22 qt.
Mixing Ratio	
Mobil Oil	
Spindle Oil	8:2
Diameter x Width	
Front	7.1 x 1.2 in.
Rear	7.1 x 1.2 in.

8

SPECIFICATIONS, MODEL A7SS

DIMENSIONS
Overall Length	78.7 in.
Overall Width	31.9 in.
Overall Height	43.5 in.
Wheelbase	51.0 in.
Road Clearance	6.7 in.
Dry Weight	329.0 lb.

PERFORMANCE
Maximum Speed	109 mph
Fuel Consumption	80 mpg
Climbing Ability	40°
Braking Distance	39 ft/31 mph
Minimum Turning Radius	86.6 in.

ENGINE
Type	2-cycle, 2 cylinder
Bore x Stroke	2.44 x 2.21 in.
Displacement	20.63 cu. in. (338cc)
Compression Ratio	7.0:1
Maximum Horsepower	42 hp/8,000 rpm
Maximum Torque ft-lb/rpm	3.99/7,000

VALVE TIMING
Inlet		
Open BTC	112°	
Close ATC	65°	
Scavenging		
Open BBC	60°	
Close ABC	60°	
Exhaust		
Open BBC	91°	
Close ABC	91°	
Carburetor Type	(2) VM28SC	
Fuel Tank Capacity	3.5 gal.	
Lubrication System	Injecto lube Oil Injection	
Engine Oil	2-stroke engine oil	
Oil Tank Capacity	2.4 qt.	
Starting System	Kickstarter	
Ignition System	Battery and Coil	
Ignition Type	Conventional/C.D.I.	
Ignition Timing (before TDC)	23°	25°

(continued)

SPECIFICATIONS, MODEL A7SS (continued)		
SPARK PLUG		
NGK	B-9HC	—
Hitachi	—	—
Denso	—	—
Champion	L60T	UL-19V
Autolite	—	—
Bosch	W340T16	—
KLG	F290	—
Lodge	R-50	—
TRANSMISSION		
Type	5-speed, constant mesh, return change	
GEAR RATIO		
Low	2.50	
2nd	1.53	
3rd	1.13	
4th	0.92	
5th	0.78	
Primary Reduction Ratio	3.40 (51/15)	
Final Reduction Ratio	2.40 (36/15)	
Overall Drive Ratio	6.36	
Transmission Oil	SAE 30	
Transmission Oil Capacity	1.27 qt.	
CLUTCH		
Type	Heavy duty multiple disk, Wet plate	
ELECTRICAL EQUIPMENT		
Generator		
Made by	Kokusan	Mitsubishi
Type	EN8	AM2010A
Regulator		
Made by	Kokusan	Mitsubishi
Type	ZR905	RL2128T
Ignition Coil		
Made by	Diamond	Diamond
Type	TU-25M-7	TU-51-1
Battery		
Type	12N 6-4A	
Capacity	12V 6AH	

8

(continued)

SPECIFICATIONS, MODEL A7SS (continued)

ELECTRICAL EQUIPMENT (continued)

Head Lamp Type	Semi-sealed beam
Head Lamp	12V, 35/25W
Tail/Brake Lamp	12V, 8/25W (4/32 cp)
Speedometer Lamp	12V, 3W
Neutral Indicator	12V, 3W
Tachometer Indicator Lamp Bulb	12V, 3W
Charge Indicator Lamp Bulb	— —
High Beam Indicator Bulb	12V, 1.5W
Turn Signal Lamp Bulb	12V, 8W

FRAME

Type	Tubular double cradle
Steering Angle	40°
Caster	63°
Trail	3.6 in.
Tire Size	
Front	3.25-18, 4PR
Rear	3.50-18, 4PR
Suspension	
Front	Telescopic Fork
Rear	Swinging Arm
Damper Stroke	
Front	4.3 in.
Rear	2.8 in.
Front Fork Oil Capacity	
(each fork)	0.22 qt.
Mixing Ratio	
Mobil Oil	
Spindle Oil	8:2
Diameter x Width	
Front	7.1 x 1.2 in.
Rear	7.1 x 1.2 in.

SPECIFICATIONS, MODEL A7R

DIMENSIONS

Overall Length	75.4 in.
Overall Width	22.8 in.
Overall Height	37.2 in.
Wheelbase	51.0 in.
Road Clearance	4.9 in.
Dry Weight	240.0 lb.

PERFORMANCE

Maximum Speed	138 mph
Fuel Consumption	—
Climbing Ability	—
Braking Distance	—
Minimum Turning Radius	150.0 in.

ENGINE

Type	2-cycle, 2 cylinder
Bore x Stroke	2.48 x 2.21 in.
Displacement	21.30 cu. in. (349cc)
Compression Ratio	7.7:1
Maximum Horsepower	53 hp/9,500
Maximum Torque ft-lb/rpm	4.04/9,500

VALVE TIMING

Inlet	
Open BTC	130°
Close ATC	70°
Scavenging	
Open BBC	63°
Close ABC	63°
Exhaust	
Open BBC	98.5°
Close ABC	98.5°
Carburetor Type	(2) M29
Fuel Tank Capacity	5.3 gal.
Lubrication System	Injecto lube and Gasoline Oil
Engine Oil	(15:1) Mixing
Oil Tank Capacity	1.05 qt.
Starting System	Push or Kick
Ignition System	Magneto
Ignition Type	Conventional
Ignition Timing (before TDC)	27° —

8

(continued)

SPECIFICATIONS, MODEL A7R (continued)	
SPARK PLUG	
NGK	B-10N —
Hitachi	— —
Denso	— —
Champion	L-55T —
Autolite	AE403 —
Bosch	W370T16 —
KLG	— —
Lodge	— —
TRANSMISSION	
Type	5-speed, constant mesh, return change
GEAR RATIO	
Low	2.06 (33/16)
2nd	1.47 (28/19)
3rd	1.18 (26/22)
4th	1.00 (24/24)
5th	0.89 (23/26)
Primary Reduction Ratio	3.35 (57/17)
Final Reduction Ratio	1.81 (29/16)
Overall Drive Ratio	5.38
Transmission Oil	SAE 10W30
Transmission Oil Capacity	1.27 qt.
CLUTCH	
Type	Heavy duty multiple disk, Wet plate
ELECTRICAL EQUIPMENT	
Generator	
Made by	Kokusan
Type	EN04
Regulator	
Made by	—
Type	—
Ignition Coil	
Made by	Kokusan
Type	ST-70
Battery	
Type	—
Capacity	—
Head Lamp Type	Semi-sealed beam

(continued)

SPECIFICATIONS, MODEL A7R (continued)	
FRAME	
Type	Tubular, double cradle
Steering Angle	40°
Caster	63°
Trail	3.6 in.
Tire Size	
Front	2.75-18, 4PR
Rear	3.00-18, 4PR
Suspension	
Front	Telescopic Fork
Rear	Swinging Arm
Damper Stroke	
Front	4.7 in.
Rear	2.8 in.
Front Fork Oil Capacity	
(each fork)	0.24 qt.
Mixing Ratio	
Mobil Oil	
Spindle Oil	8:2
Diameter x Width	
Front	7.9 x 0.8 in.
Rear	7.1 x 1.4 in.

INDEX

9

9

MAINTENANCE LOG

DATE	TYPE OF SERVICE	COST	REMARKS

MAINTENANCE LOG

DATE	TYPE OF SERVICE	COST	REMARKS

NOTES

Owner-Service...
for Imported Cars and Trucks

Clymer's professionally-written car manuals are a must for every do-it-yourself car owner. Expert text by top technical writers is illustrated by hundreds of photos, drawings, and diagrams. The use of special tools and test equipment is avoided wherever possible. When necessary, these items are illustrated in actual use or alone. Jobs that are not within the ability of the owner/mechanic are pointed out and service referred to a dealer or repair shop.

The manuals listed below offer complete maintenance, troubleshooting, tune-up, and overhaul information for hundreds of different models (Mercedes covers tune-up only). They are available through local bookstores, automotive accessories outlets, or postpaid directly from Clymer Publications.

• *NEW COLOR-IDENTIFIED QUICK REFERENCE PAGES* will be included in most new and updated books. The most frequently used specs will be found all together at the front of the book for ready reference — including tune-up specs, fluid capacities, torque settings, light bulb types, tire pressures, adjustments, and more.

• *NEW TAB IDENTIFIERS* will be included in all new and updated books to help readers locate chapters and sections easily.

VOLKSWAGEN BEETLE, SUPER BEETLE, KARMANN GHIA, 1961-1977	(A103)	$8.00
VOLKSWAGEN RABBIT AND SCIROCCO, 1975-1977	(A122)	$9.00
VOLKSWAGEN PERFORMANCE TUNING, 1200-1700cc ENGINES, 1961-1973	(A128)	$9.00
VOLKSWAGEN TRANSPORTER, 1961-1976	(A110)	$9.00
VOLKSWAGEN TYPE 3, 1962-1973	(A120)	$9.00
VOLKSWAGEN DASHER, 1974-1977	(A121)	$9.00
VOLKSWAGEN 411 & 412, 1968-1974	(A125)	$9.00
AUDI FOX, 1973-1977	(A132)	$9.00
AUDI 100LS, 1970-1976	(A131)	$9.00
BMW 1600 & 2002, 1967-1976	(A138)	$9.00
CAPRI, 1970-1976	(A143)	$9.00
DATSUN 510, 610, & 710, 1968-1976	(A149)	$9.00
DATSUN 1200 & B210, 1971-1976	(A151)	$9.00
DATSUN 240, 260, & 280Z, 1970-1976	(A152)	$9.00
DATSUN L521, PL521, & PL620 PICKUPS, 1968-1977	(A148)	$9.00
DODGE COLT, 1971-1977	(A154)	$9.00
FIAT 124, 1967-1977	(A156)	$9.00
FIAT 128 AND X1/9, 1971-1977	(A157)	$9.00
*FIAT 131, 1975-1977	(A158)	$9.00
*FORD COURIER PICKUPS, 1972-1977	(A172)	$9.00
*HONDA ACCORD, 1976-1977	(A228)	$9.00
HONDA CIVIC, 1973-1976	(A227)	$9.00
JAGUAR 3.8 & 4.2 E-TYPE	(A225)	$10.00
MAZDA RX-2 & RX-3, 1971-1974	(A164)	$9.00
MERCEDES-BENZ TUNE-UP, 1958-1976	(A180)	$10.00
MGA/MGB & GT, 1956-1976	(A165)	$9.00
OPEL GT, KADETT, 1900, MANTA, 1966-1977	(A175)	$9.00
PORSCHE 911 & 912, 1965-1976	(A183)	$10.00
PORSCHE 914 & 914/6, 1970-1975	(A184)	$10.00
SAAB 95, 96, 99, & SONETT, 1967-1976	(A185)	$9.00
SPRITE/MG MIDGET, 1958-1977	(A205)	$9.00
SUBARU 1400 & 1600cc, 1972-1977	(A186)	$9.00
TOYOTA COROLLA & CARINA, 1968-1976	(A198)	$9.00
TOYOTA CORONA, MARK II, CELICA, CROWN, STOUT, & HI-LUX, 1968-1976	(A191)	$9.00
TRIUMPH TR2-TR6 & GT6, 1954-1976	(A210)	$9.00
VOLVO 122S & P1800, 1962-1968	(A220)	$9.00
VOLVO 140 & 240 SERIES, 1967-1976	(A221)	$9.00

*Early 1978 publication

CLYMER PUBLICATIONS

**222 North Virgil Avenue
Los Angeles, California 90004**

Do-It-Yourself Boat Maintenance

The world's largest publisher of automotive and motorcycle manuals now offers a complete line of maintenance and tune-up handbooks for owners of sailboats, powerboats, outboard motors, stern drive units, and small inboard engines.

Each title features step-by-step procedures for maintaining and repairing the hull, fittings, interior, electrical systems, plumbing, galley equipment, and the countless other items that keep boat owners busy.

As in all Clymer handbooks, the expert text and detailed photos and illustrations will put money-saving maintenance well within the reach of anyone reasonably handy with tools.

The titles listed below are available through your local bookstore, marine outlet, or postpaid direct from Clymer Publications.

SAILBOAT MAINTENANCE . . . . (B600) $9.00

POWERBOAT MAINTENANCE . . . . (B620) $9.00

BRITISH SEAGULL OUTBOARDS, 2 TO 6 HP . . . . . . (B660) $8.00

CHRYSLER OUTBOARDS, 3.5 TO 20 HP,
1966-1975 . . . . (B655) $8.00

CHRYSLER OUTBOARDS, 25 TO 135 HP,
1966-1977 . . . . (B657) $8.00

EVINRUDE OUTBOARDS, 1.5 TO 33 HP,
1965-1975 . . . . (B644) $8.00

EVINRUDE OUTBOARDS, 40 TO 135 HP,
1965-1975 . . . . (B647) $8.00

JOHNSON OUTBOARDS, 40 TO 135 HP,
1965-1975 . . . . (B665) $8.00

MERCURY OUTBOARDS, 3.9 TO 40 HP,
1964-1975 . . . . (B650) $8.00

MERCURY OUTBOARDS, 50 TO 175 HP,
1964-1977 . . . . (B653) $8.00

SAILBOAT AUXILIARY ENGINES (Atomic, Chrysler,
Ford, Perkins, Pisces, Volvo-Penta,
Westerbeke, and Yanmar) . . . . (B610) $9.00

STERN DRIVE UNITS (OMC, MerCruiser, Volvo,
Stern-Powr, Berkeley, and Jacuzzi) . . . . (B641) $9.00

CLYMER PUBLICATIONS

222 NORTH VIRGIL AVENUE • LOS ANGELES, CALIFORNIA 90004